How to Write Computer Documentation for Users

Second Edition

How to Write Computer Documentation for Users

Second Edition

SUSAN J. GRIMM

 VAN NOSTRAND REINHOLD
_____ *New York*

Copyright © 1987 by Van Nostrand Reinhold

Library of Congress Catalog Card Number 86–10989

ISBN 0–442–23228–4

This book was first published in 1982 under the title *How to Write Computer Manuals for Users*

Van Nostrand Reinhold
115 Fifth Avenue
New York, New York 10003

Van Nostrand Reinhold International Company Limited
11 New Fetter Lane
London EC4P 4EE, England

Van Nostrand Reinhold
480 La Trobe Street
Melbourne, Victoria 3000, Australia

Macmillan of Canada
Division of Canada Publishing Corporation
164 Commander Boulevard
Agincourt, Ontario M1S 3C7, Canada

16 15 14 13 12 11 10 9 8 7 6 5 4

Library of Congress Cataloging-in-Publication Data

Grimm, Susan J.
    How to write computer documentation for users.
    Rev. ed. of: How to write computer manuals for users.
    Includes bibliographical references and index.
    1. Electronic data processing—Authorship.
2. Computers—Handbooks, manuals, etc. 3. Technical writing. I. Grimm, Susan J. How to write computer manuals for users. II. Title.
QA76.165.G74   1986   808'.066004   86–10989
ISBN 0–442–23228–4

Short Contents

Contents

PART II WHEN YOU WRITE

PART III AFTER YOU WRITE

Checklists

Examples

Preface

WHO THE BOOK IS FOR

This book is for all writers of user documentation, whether those writers are systems analysts, programmers, or technical writers. All user documentation writers will find practical, step-by-step procedures and advice if they follow this book sequentially. In addition, technical writers will find useful ideas on researching the subject and presenting the material. Systems analysts and programmers will be able to interpret the technical aspects of the system into language that will help the user understand and use the application system described.

Writers for all kinds of computers—mainframes, minis, micros, PC's—and all kinds of application systems—batch, online, timesharing—should find this book useful. All computer systems have common elements. All take data (input), do something with it (operations, calculations), and produce results (output). In traditional batch systems, input, operations, and output are clearly defined tasks. In online and microcomputer systems, the distinction is blurred, but the distinction still exists. While the book focuses on business applications, the principles it gives apply to any system from computer games to sophisticated business applications.

Although the book will be most helpful to the inexperienced writer, experienced writers can also find good ideas and new approaches. The book not only tells writers what to do, it tells them what not to do. Thus, both experienced and inexperienced writers can avoid common pitfalls that hinder user understanding. This book will help all writers research, plan, write, review, produce, and maintain successful user documentation. It provides much-needed information for an important, but often overlooked, area of the data processing industry. Very little formal training is available in this field; this book answers a need.

Good user documentation cuts costs, especially for software vendors. Following the advice and procedures in this book, writers can produce documentation that will save users time.

Faster training and easily accessible information save users' time. Fewer phone calls or meetings to answer users' questions save time in the Data Processing Department or software development company.

The book's emphasis is on writing manuals or printed documentation. However, the same principles apply to developing online user documentation and using documentation generators or processors. Sections 5 and 6 and parts of other sections will not apply if your documentation is online.

FEATURES OF THE BOOK

This book gives practical procedures that make documentation easier and quicker to write. Its main feature is that *it thoroughly details the process of producing documentation.* In addition, its features include the following.

- A step-by-step system for planning and writing
- Chronological format—from researching the subject, to planning the documentation, to writing the text, to keeping the documentation up to date
- Practical advice for the writing process—how to write a manual that is easy to read and use
- Checklists—steps to follow for each stage of development process
- Examples and illustrations—"how to do it" for each stage of planning and writing
- Alternative methods and "when to use" advice—writers can adapt the methods to fit specific systems and situations

I hope that you will find this book a useful tool in your work. I welcome hearing from readers who may have suggestions or recommendations that may make this book even more useful in a revision.

Susan J. Grimm

What User Documentation Should Do

How can you make the "magic" of a computer understandable to people who know little or nothing about computers? This book shows how to research, plan, write, edit, review, produce, and maintain user documentation that explains computer systems. Such documentation takes the mystery out of computer systems. It tells people who don't have computer backgrounds how to understand something that they need to know.

Focus on the Users

Computers touch all of us in many ways; they affect virtually every aspect of business in every industry. Personal computers have changed many businesses and some homes. Desks are often called "workstations" now. Computers have blurred the distinction between the "smokestack" industries and the "high tech" industries.

Computers solve problems, handle data, entertain, and help make decisions. Computers affect our personal lives every time we go to a bank or make a purchase in a department store or make a plane reservation. So we are all computer users. This book shows how to explain computer use to those who deal directly with computer input or output.

User documentation must overcome users' apprehension, build confidence, and provide easy-to-follow instructions. The goal is to enable users to prepare and enter their data and use the computer output. The most important ingredient in the process of developing user documentation is the user. After all, if the users of a system are afraid of it or don't understand it, the system cannot achieve its intended purpose. The best system ever developed is worthless if it is not used properly. Users must understand that the computer system is really theirs, designed to solve their problems and meet their needs.

Microcomputers and personal computers (the term "microcomputer" in this book will refer to personal computers as well as small business computers) have expanded the number of computer users. Computers used to be the property of data processing departments. Now computer terminals and personal computers are in many offices and homes. These new users, especially, require excellent and thorough documentation. They are often working alone with their microcomputers. Because they are new and have no one readily available to help them, microcomputer users will be less tolerant of inadequate documentation.

The discussion of microcomputer systems in this book usually refers to software packages purchased for the microcomputer. However, microcomputer users also can develop their programs because of the easy-to-use program generators available. They can use the principles in this book to develop their own documentation should they choose to do so.

People responsible for supporting a company's microcomputers via an information center are also responsible for providing user documentation. Microcomputers can also be part of a network and serve as data entry points to large, mainframe computers. In these cases, the explanations in this book of batch and online systems would apply.

Use Clear Writing

The last thing users want to read is computer jargon. Jargon turns them off and hinders their understanding of computer systems. In many industries, consumers are now demanding clear writing so they can understand what they're getting into. Legal documents and insurance policies are being written in clearer language as a result. The same is true in the computer industry.

Writing style becomes important in light of that goal. Documentation that is thorough, technically correct, grammatically perfect, and well-designed is still ineffective if the readers get lost in the text. Therefore, writing style must be adapted to insure understanding.

Before you go any further, forget some of what your high school English teachers taught about conclusions, vocabulary variety, formal language, and complex and compound sentences. You don't have to be able to diagram sentences or name gerunds and infinitives to be a good writer of user documentation. Remember, however, the basics of writing: sentence structure, noun/verb agreement, spelling, and punctuation.

This may seem strange advice from a former English teacher. The user documentation's goal is to explain a system, not to impress the reader. This book will show that some of the techniques that get A's in high school English may be completely inappropriate for writing good instructions.

Be Accurate and Effective

Although clear writing is vitally important, thorough research and planning are also essential. They give you the knowledge and background to write clearly. You cannot write about what you don't understand. Editing and review insure technical accuracy and grammatical correctness. They must be done systematically and completely.

Examples, graphics, checklists, and summaries all help your reader understand the topic. This book explains what to use and when to use it effectively.

Keeping a documentation up-to-date is a challenge to any writer. This book offers suggestions for maintaining documentation once it's released.

The text or the words of printed user documentation are only part of your task. The manual must also be printed (or copied) and distributed. This book explains how to plan and be involved in producing the user documentation.

Study the examples in this book. They'll help you become a good writer of user documentation. This book wasn't written to turn you into a Shakespeare or even a Harold Robbins. Its goal is to help you help computer users.

PART I

Before You Write

Before you can write anything, you must first know what you are writing about, for whom you are writing, and how you are going to write. Architects don't just start building houses. They first determine what the owners want and what materials are available. Only then can the next step begin. A writer must follow similar steps.

Before you write, you must obtain background information (Section 1) and plan the documentation (Section 2).

Obtain Background Information

Gather your information before you write. That means know about the computer system and know about the user of that system. Such research is essential if you are to achieve your goal of explaining a specific computer application system to specific users.

This section will help with any system but is aimed at *new* systems. Writing can begin as soon as the basic system design is completed. Perhaps this is an ideal. Often, especially for in-house systems, the need for user documentation becomes apparent only after a system is released and the users can't understand it. Regardless of when writing begins, or whether the system is old or new, the steps are basically the same. You must understand the computer system (Chapter 1), understand the users (Chapter 2), and compare your knowledge of the system and of the users (Chapter 3).

1

Understand the Computer System

Obviously, writers have to understand their topics. Therefore, your first task is to find out what the application program does. It is not essential, however, that you know the technical details about the program's coding or the sequence of operations.

If you are a programmer or have programming experience, this phase will be easier for you than it will be for someone who does not have a technical background. Programmers can read the code and find out about a program. However, even those without a technical background can understand the system. They must do a little more research, though. (The non-technical person will have an advantage in the second part of obtaining background information, Chapter 2, Understand the Users.)

Your goals for this phase of obtaining background information can be summarized by the following checklist.

Checklist for Obtaining System Information

1. What is the purpose of the application system?
2. What user need does it fulfill?
3. What data does it require?
4. Where do the data come from?
5. How do the data enter the computer?
6. What does the computer check about the data (numeric, alphabetic, size, etc.)?
7. What data must be present? In what format?
8. What data items are optional?

9. How and where are data items stored? For how long?

10. What are the relationships among various kinds of data?

11. What commands are acceptable? When are they acceptable?

12. What calculations and functions does the program perform?

13. What outputs are produced?

14. How is output requested?

15. What does the user do with the output?

The answers to these questions can vary greatly. The purpose of the application system can be anything from an order entry system to computer graphics. Because the purposes can be so different, the data, input, and output can cover a wide range.

For microcomputer users, some of these questions may not even apply. For example, creating and storing the data and output may be at the discretion of the users. All that the user documentation can do is suggest or recommend procedures and options.

To answer the questions listed above when you're writing documentation for an in-house application, you have two good sources of information: the programmer or systems analyst and the system documentation. If the system is in the planning phase, its documentation may be functional specifications and, possibly, program specifications.

Because of the many people writing packaged software for microcomputers, you have no guarantee that functional specifications and/or program specifications exist. The existence or non-existence of these documents may depend on who is developing the package and whether the developer is doing it alone or for a company that produces such packages and requires development documentation.

Many programmers develop packages and write their own user documentation. If you are one of those people, use the suggestions in this chapter as a checklist for items to consider when writing the user documentation.

Talk to Programmers

Your first source of information is the programmer or systems analyst. Some computer installations have the writer involved with the project during the design phase. This has the advantage of giving you a great deal of background information. However, it may be too time-consuming, especially if an installation has many systems and only one writer. This section explains how to learn about the system after it has been designed.

The people who are designing and coding the programs can be a big help to you. If the system is large, many programmers may be coding smaller parts of the system. They themselves may not know what the entire system does or the interrelationships of all the programs that make up a system. In these situations, you must first talk to the project leader or systems analyst responsible for the entire system. Later, programmers responsible for the individual programs can help you answer specific questions. Use the checklist at the beginning of this chapter as a basis for your interview.

Even if you are not a programmer, learn enough computer jargon to be able to converse with the technical people. It will make it easier for you to gain their cooperation. But don't be afraid to ask questions when you're not sure about something. Although programmers often don't enjoy writing, they are usually very happy to explain the system to the writer to make things easier for the user. Often, however, programmers are under pressure to get the system completed. They may feel they are being paid to program, not to talk to you. Therefore, it is a good idea to get the express endorsement from the project leader for the time involved in interviewing programmers.

Get as much written material as possible. The project leader may have memos, flowcharts, sample input forms, report layouts, error messages that the program prints, and other materials that will help you understand the system. Take notes during your interviews. Don't think about the final form or organization of the documentation yet. Once you've gathered everything, you can put it into logical categories.

Checklist for Talking to Programmers

1. Talk with the person who knows the entire system and has been involved with the system's development from the beginning. This person is likely to be in the middle somewhere, not at the bottom or the top of the department or project

team organization. This will help you understand the basic system, its purpose, the flow of information, the sequence of events, etc.

2. Talk with programmers working on individual programs for information about error messages and other input or output. Get a list of possible user errors. They will explain what the program expects.

3. Take good notes. Get as much previously written information as you can, such as

Flowcharts

Program messages

Functional or program specifications

Read the Functional Specifications

Most computer installations require that systems be planned in great detail before actual coding begins. The exact nature of the plan depends on the installation. Many use functional specifications or detailed design as part of the documentation for the system's design. Some systems begin with a general design and/or a requirements definition. These documents are valuable to the manual writer, but the functional specifications provide more detail. Functional specifications are written plans that show clearly how the programs operate on the user's data to produce the desired results. Thus, the functional specifications help you understand the system.

Although you won't use all of the functional specifications in the user documentation, read these specifications thoroughly to learn about the system. Don't plan or outline the documentation yet. Later, adapt what you learn to the user documentation.

Functional specifications often contain the following parts:

System overview

Data dictionary

Input description

Operation description

Calculations

Output description

File description

Other information

Since different installations have different standards, and different methods for presenting their functional specifications, the parts of the functional specifications explained here will not apply to every situation. Unfortunately, no standard way to write the functional specifications exists. But some of the parts should apply, and all of them should help you adapt the material available to you.

The following subsections explain some of the parts that are typically found in functional specifications. When you understand what information is available in the functional specifications, you will know what to look for and what parts will be most helpful in writing the user documentation.

System Overview   Many functional specifications begin with a system summary or overview. This part of the functional specifications:

1. Defines the system's objectives.

2. Explains the system's capabilities and computations.

3. Summarizes input forms and methods.

4. Summarizes system operation.

5. Summarizes output.

6. Summarizes the system's effects.

7. Explains what the system will not do.

Study the system overview of the functional specifications carefully. It is the easiest part to understand and a good place to start. It will give you a good idea of the whole concept of the system.

For example, a company called Acme Distributing Company distributes widgets, gadgets, gismos, and thing-a-majigs. The company wants to develop a purchase order/inventory system. A simplified system overview for that system is shown in Example 1.1. (The Acme Distributing Company's purchase order/inventory system serves as a case study for this book. Examples of the in-house application are based on this system.)

Example 1.1   System Overview—In-House Application

The Acme Distributing Company's purchase order/inventory system will keep track of purchase orders. When the merchandise is received, the system will maintain the number and value of items in inventory.

Order clerks will complete the purchase order input form that lists:

Purchase order number

Date

Supplier company

Item

Quantity

Cost

When merchandise is received, receiving clerks will complete an input form that lists:

Purchase order number

Date

Supplier company

Item

Quantity

Cost

Invoice number

Check number

When this merchandise is sold, sales clerks will complete an input form that lists:

Date

Item sold

Quantity

Amount

All of the input forms will be sent to the Data Entry Department where the data will be entered into the computer.

The computer will edit all the information for completeness and correctness. It will store the data in two files:

Purchase order file

Inventory file

When items ordered arrive, the purchase order record will be noted with the message RECEIVED. The merchandise received increases the inventory file. When items are sold, the inventory file decreases.

When the amount of an item in inventory falls below a predetermined level, the computer will note this and print a report to be used for re-ordering.

The system will compute the total cost of goods sold and compare it with sales income.

The system will produce the following reports:

Purchase orders listed by purchase order number

Purchase orders by date

Purchase orders by supplier

Purchase orders by item

Purchase orders received by item

Purchase orders received by check number

Purchase orders received by invoice number

Purchase orders received by supplier

Inventory items for reorder

Cost of items in inventory

Sales income from items sold

Cost compared with sales income

The application system in this first case study is relatively simple and is an in-house application. Many application systems will be more complicated. This is especially true of sophisticated computer graphics applications like CAD/CAM (computer-aided design/computer-aided manufacturing) systems. However, a simple application serves best for an illustration. The system overview would be similar whether the application is batch or online or whether it is for a microcomputer or a mainframe.

The second case study is a typical microcomputer application, a spreadsheet. This case study involves a spreadsheet package called Wonder-Calc. A system overview of this package is given in Example 1.2. (The Wonder-Calc spreadsheet is fictitious and serves as a case study illustrating microcomputer systems in this book.)

Example 1.2   System Overview—Microcomputer Application

> Wonder-Calc is an electronic spreadsheet or worksheet. It replaces traditional methods of calculation and overcomes the limitations of paper worksheets. Wonder-Calc remembers the relationships among the entries and automatically calculates and recalculates based on user-defined formulas.
>
> Typical uses of Wonder-Calc are budgeting for small businesses and personal finances, analyzing production or sales, planning personal investments, developing financial worksheets, and performing "what if" calculations (If I change this number, what will happen?).
>
> Wonder-Calc's basic format is a grid of rows and columns. The maximum size of the grid is 250 rows long and 60 columns wide.
>
> You use this grid to set up your worksheets. Enter:
>
> words
>
> numbers
>
> formulas
>
> Words are headings or titles. Numbers are in the format you define (dollar amounts with two decimal places, percentages, etc.). You determine your own formulas on the basis of the calculations you wish to perform.
>
> Wonder-Calc is an interactive system. You communicate with Wonder-Calc through commands (COPY, DELETE, FORMAT, INSERT, MOVE, PRINT, etc.).

System overviews such as these provide an outline for your research (not necessarily for the documentation). From it, you have a basic understanding of the system and what it does. Further research will supply the details. Many details will be in other parts of the functional specifications. Other details will come from interviews with programmers and users.

Data Dictionary   All systems require facts and figures that enter the system. These facts and figures are called data. The system calculates, manipulates, or interprets the data to produce information that is meaningful to the user.

Although microcomputers have some structured systems, often microcomputer users define their own data. They determine the names, lengths, format, and meaning of the data they will use. Therefore, a microcomputer package like Wonder-Calc will not have a data dictionary that applies to the user.

However, a large business system, like Acme's purchase order/inventory system, will have defined data with required lengths and formats for these data. This is true whether the system is batch or online.

The functional specifications should list all of the data that enter the system or are produced by it. One way of doing this is a data dictionary. This is a list of all the data in a system. It includes:

Data names

Abbreviations or the name that the system will use in its programs (if applicable)

Data source (input forms, computations, etc.)

Range for numerical data (the lowest and highest numbers acceptable)

Definitions or description of the data

Codes and their meanings (e.g., "M" means male; "F" means female)

For example, part of the data dictionary in the functional specifications for the purchase order/inventory system would be as shown in Example 1.3.

From this, you know that the system keeps the number of widgets and gadgets and the cost of each item. You know the maximum number for each of these. Interpreting this: We may enter any number of widgets or gadgets as long as the number does not exceed 99,999 widgets or gadgets. The computer will accept our having none. The cost of each cannot exceed $9,999.99. The computer will accept zero dollars in inventory. The system name will probably not be part of your manual, because the users will never see it.

Not all functional specifications will have a data dictionary. Then, data are described in the input or output descriptions. In

Example 1.3   Data Dictionary

Data Name	System Name	Description	Range	Source
Widgets	WID	Number of widgets ordered in inventory	0–99999	User-entered
Gadgets	GAD	Number of gadgets ordered in inventory	9–99999	User-entered
Cost per item	CST	Cost/item for any item ordered or in inventory	0.00– 9999.99	User-entered

such cases, you should make your own data dictionary. Keep a list of all the system's data. Include in that list:

Data needed

Source (user-entered or computer-generated)

Range for numeric data

Size (maximum number of characters for non-numeric data)

If ranges and sizes are not part of the functional specifications, obtain that information from people working on the system. Find out if the programs detect violations of the ranges and sizes and what happens when the programs detect violations. Since these violations of the data limitations are common causes of unexplained strange behavior by programs, users must understand the limitations so they won't be confused.

Input Description   This part of the functional specifications describes all the data that come into the system and how they are entered. Since users will be responsible for supplying these data, this part of the functional specifications is important to your research. The input description may repeat some of the information that is in the data dictionary. However, it includes only data that are entered by the user, and it is in the order that the user enters them. An input description may look like Example 1.4 when an input form is the source.

Example 1.4   Input Description

Data Name	Input Form Columns	Format	Check	Source
Date	1–6	MMDDYY	MM = 01–12 DD = 01–31 YY = 81–99	Purchase Order Input Form

This says that the date will be in the first 6 columns of the record and will contain the 2-digit month number, the day, and the last 2 digits of the year. For example, August 6, 1982 would be 080682.

Use an example of input description when you write the input form instructions of the manual. (See Chapter 13.)

The input description part of the functional specifications will vary greatly depending on the input media. If the user will enter the data on a computer terminal (online system), the input description should include the prompting messages that appear on the terminal screen to ask for the data, as in Example 1.5.

In this case, the input description explains the data name, the prompting message that asks for these data, the format that the data must take, how the computer will check the data, and the error message that will appear at the terminal if the data's format and/or content is incorrect.

Sometimes users do not use an input form or prompting messages to enter data. Instead, they create a file that contains the data to be entered. If the user will create a computer file as input, the

Example 1.5   Input Description with Prompting Message

Data Name	Terminal Prompt	Format	Check	Error
Date	ENTER DATE	MMDDYY	MM = 01–12 DD = 01–31 YY = 82–99	INVALID DATE

Example 1.6   Input Description with Input Line and Length

Line Number	Data Name	Length	Format	Check
01	Date	6	MMDDYY	MM = 01–12
				DD = 01–31
				YY = 82–99

input description will include information about the input line and length, as in Example 1.6.

For microcomputer applications, the user will almost always enter data on the microcomputer keyboard. (Of course, exceptions exist. Users may use a mouse or a light pen to enter data.) Depending on the package or user-developed software, the user may or may not receive prompting messages on the microcomputer screen. For example, Wonder-Calc presents users with rows and columns. It is up to the users to decide what data they will enter in those rows and columns and what formulas will calculate totals, etc.

Operation Description   This part of the functional specifications explains what the system will do, under what conditions, and for

Example 1.7   Operation Description—Acme's Purchase Order/Inventory System

Operation Name	Condition	System Action	Result
Add a purchase order number (P.O.).	Purchase order number must be 8 digits and not already on file. If not numeric, print P.O. NOT NUMERIC. If already on file, print P.O. ALREADY ON FILE.	Check for purchase order data.	If all data present, record updates the purchase order file.

what results. It tells you what happens to the input data entered by the user. An operation description for Acme's purchase order/inventory system may look like Example 1.7.

This tells you what the computer will look for, what will happen if it doesn't find what it needs, and what it will look for next.

How this affects the user depends upon whether the system is online or not. If it's online, the computer will check the entered data items right away and accept or reject them. Sometimes, if the data items are unacceptable, an error message prints immediately, allowing correction. Other times, the program stops as soon as it encounters an error. Then, the user must determine the cause of the error and start over. Find out how the system will treat errors.

In systems that are not online, the computer will print an edit report that lists rejected data with error messages. Either way, the user has to know why the entry was incorrect and how to correct it. Therefore, the operations description will help you write the operating instructions or processing section of the documentation. (See Chapter 14.)

Many online systems restrict users' access to certain data. Since this will affect the user's view of the system operation, the user documentation must explain what data the user can access and what the user can do with these data (look at them, change them, change them but not delete them, etc.).

The operation descriptions of microcomputer packages are often different. The user probably determines what the operations will be by using different commands. Therefore, the functional specifications, if they exist, should explain all the possibilities. An operation description for Wonder-Calc may look like Example 1.8. (This example does not include all the possible operations that could be found in this kind of a package.)

Calculations   This part of the functional specifications explains the formulas used in the system. Usually, packaged microcomputer packages allow the users to determine their own calculations. But most large business systems perform some "number crunching." Of course, application systems often do a lot more than calculate numbers. However, calculations, when they are part of the system, are important. You must understand them. A calculation may look like Example 1.9.

Example 1.8   Operation Description—Wonder-Calc

Wonder-Calc allows the user to determine which operations to perform. Many commands have sub-commands which offer variations of the main command. The following commands are available.

Command	Sub-Command	User Enters	Operation
COPY		C	Copies data, formats, or formulas from one row or column into another row or column
	COPY ACROSS	C,A	Copies the data into columns to their right
	COPY DOWN	C,D	Copies the data into rows below them
DELETE		D	Deletes rows and columns; closes the space
	DELETE ROW	D,R	Deletes a row
	DELETE COLUMN	D,C	Deletes a column
INSERT		I	Inserts new rows or columns
	INSERT ROW	I,R	Inserts a row
	INSERT COLUMN	I,C	Inserts a column

Example 1.9   Calculation—Acme's Purchase Order/Inventory System

TOTAL COST = CST × QUANTITY

Example 1.10   Calculations—Wonder-Calc

Users use formulas and functions to determine the calculations Wonder-Calc will perform. Users create formulas by moving the cursor to the areas to be calculated, separating each area with the appropriate mathematical operation sign (=, −, /, ×).

Functions also calculate Wonder-Calc figures:

Add (*row or column*) adds the values in a row or column.

Average (*row or column*) averages the values in a row or column.

This will help you understand how the system generates numbers for output. As we will see in the next chapter, users may or may not be interested in an explanation of the calculations.

The calculation section for a microcomputer package explains the possibilities. Example 1.10 illustrates Wonder-Calc's capabilities.

Output Description   This part of the functional specifications describes the output. Output takes a variety of forms: paper, screen, magnetic tape, microfiche, etc. The functional specifications will explain the kinds of output available.

The output of a microcomputer package depends on the package being used. Usually, the user decides the size and format of the data appearing as output. If microcomputer use and applications are standardized within a company, the output description can be similar to the output descriptions for large, in-house systems.

The output description identifies which data elements appear in which output. The output is the result of the system's operations and calculations. An output description may look like Example 1.11.

Example 1.11   Output Description

Item	Quantity	Amount/Item	Total
XXXXXXXXXXX	99999	9999.99	9999999.99

Example 1.12   Actual Output

Item	Quantity	Amount/Item	Total
WIDGET	10	25.00	250.00

Computer personnel usually use X's to denote alphabetic data and 9's to denote numeric data. Thus, you know that the actual report will look like Example 1.12.

This is something that is meaningful to the users. You will use this information when you write the output descriptions. (See Chapter 15.)

File Description   This part of the functional specifications describes the purpose, content, use, and structure of the data files. A file description may look like Example 1.13.

This can help you understand the data stored and used by the system. However, it is rather technical. Users, especially users of batch systems, are not interested in such technical details. Even users of online systems, unless they name and control their own files, will not be concerned with the file description.

Therefore, if you are able to interpret the information, use this part of the functional specifications to enhance your own understanding of the system. Don't use the file description to write the user documentation unless the files are visible to the user.

A data base may store the data on the basis of relationships among data items or on the basis of a hierarchy of the data items. While users do not need to know the operational details of the

Example 1.13   File Description

File name:	INV001
Description:	Random binary
	Disk
	Read only
Purpose:	Contains items in inventory

data base management system (DBMS), they should understand the basic concepts of a data base and how it structures their data. Users need more details to use data base packages on a microcomputer, especially if they are creating their own applications using a data base. For large data bases on mainframe computers, users must understand what data are shared among many users and what data are their own.

Other Information   As stated earlier, functional specifications vary from one computer installation to another. Many functional specifications include decision tables. They explain logical requirements and relationships by listing all possible conditions and actions. The decisions they represent affect system operation.

If you are not familiar with decision tables, *Data Processing Documentation* by William Harper can help you understand them. (See *Further References* at the end of this chapter.)

User procedures are sometimes included in the functional specifications. These provide a summary of the procedures the user normally follows to use the system. Although these procedures are only an overview, they can form a basis for the detailed manual you must write.

Specifications for online systems should include the messages that will appear on the user's terminal. Of course, you will need to know and understand these so you can explain them to the user.

Read the Program Specifications

After you've read and studied the functional specifications, read the program specifications if they are available. Program specifications translate the functional specifications into the functioning of the system. They are computer-related to explain the "how" of the system. They describe the distinct, separate tasks that the system must perform. Program specifications include design and logic requirements, program flowcharts, the purpose of each program, and other programming details.

Since they are technical, program specifications will not be as much help to you in writing because users will not be concerned with technical programming details. However, if you have the technical knowledge to understand them, you should read them. They will give you a better understanding of the system. The better you understand the system, the easier it will be for you to write.

Read about the Technology Involved

Sometimes you may need to know more about the technology involved in the system. This is especially true when the subject involves a new application using new technology. For example, the area of computer graphics is a rapidly changing field. When it first appeared, it was geared toward the engineering audience and was very complicated. Now it is available with many microcomputer software packages. The plotters needed to print computer graphics are becoming more commonplace. Consequently, you must keep up with the technology as it changes. (See *Further References* at the end of this chapter.)

The same is true for any field that uses computers in a specialized way for specialized results. Voice communication, telecommunications, and many others are areas that require a little more research on the part of the writer.

Summary   Remember that, at this stage of development, you are gathering information. Don't try to plan or write the documentation until this stage is complete and until you do research about the users also.

Your best sources for obtaining information about the system are programmers and the functional specifications. Program specifications will add to your own understanding of the system, but the information in these will probably not interest the user.

If the system already exists, the best research is to use the system yourself. You can find out first hand the idiosyncrasies of the system and understand it well. By using the system yourself, you become the user.

Further References

Burton, Philip E. *A Dictionary of Microcomputing.* New York: Garland Publishing, Inc., 1976.

If you write manuals for microcomputers, a rapidly growing market, this reference will help.

Harper, William L. *Data Processing Documentation: Standards, Procedures, and Applications.* Englewood Cliffs, New Jersey: Prentice-Hall, Inc., 1981.
The "Decision Logic Tables" chapter explains how to use decision tables. Other sections, such as the one about system flowcharts, will also be helpful.

Ralston, Anthony, editor, and Meek, Chester L., assistant editor. *Encyclopedia of Computer Science.* New York: Petrocelli/Charter, 1976.

Sippl, Charles J., and Sippl, Roger J. *Computer Dictionary and Handbook.* Indianapolis: H. W. Sams and Co., Inc., 1978.
Writers without a technical background need a dictionary of computer terms to help them understand programmers and functional specifications. This book also provides explanations of basic computer concepts.

2

Understand the Users

Understanding the reader is probably the most important quality of any writer. This is especially true for writing user documentation. Writers without a technical background have an advantage in this area. It's easy to understand the users' frustration with computer terms and their bewilderment about what the computer really does.

Before you can write, you must know who the users are, how they will use the documentation, and what the system can do to help them perform their jobs. Your knowledge and understanding of the user will determine the language, scope, and detail of the documentation.

To gain an understanding of the users and the requirements:

Define the users.

Determine the users' needs.

Talk to the users.

Determine the uses of the documentation.

Decide the scope of the documentation.

Decide the language of the documentation.

Define the Users

Users come in many varieties. Their numbers are growing. As computers become more commonplace, people with little or no previous exposure to computers now use them. Even children who play video games are computer users; video games use programs and computer graphics. Executives who thought only secretaries had keyboards on their desks now want information from the computer on their desktop terminals or computers. Data Processing Department personnel no longer have total control over the users or even the data. Thus, defining a system's users is not always simple.

The cost of small business computers is decreasing. More companies are buying them. Software developers come up with new applications constantly. People in companies with their own computers are demanding new information. People are buying personal computers for their homes; they need to know how to use them.

A user is anyone who has anything to do with a computer system. People who prepare data, manipulate data, interpret output, or operate a computer terminal are all users.

First put your readers into the appropriate category.

Purchasers of packaged software

Clients for whom special systems have been developed

Purchasers of small computers (including home computers)

Users in your own company

Users who prepare input

Users who operate a computer terminal

Users who see only the reports but are not involved in entering data

Further define the users by the industry or application:

Engineers

Accountants

Home users (including players of computer games)

Users of medical modeling and diagnostic systems

Marketing personnel

Navigators

Military personnel

Meteorologists

Politicians and political forecasters

Artists

Aviators

Police and other law enforcement personnel

School personnel (instruction and reporting systems)

Scientists

Theater personnel (movies and lighting by computers)

Repairpersons

Musicians

The list could go on; it grows constantly. As new applications are designed, more and more people become users.

After defining the users' category and industry, define the users' levels:

Professionals

Executives

Managers

Home users

Secretaries

Clerical personnel

People outside the user company who see reports

Word processing operators

Your job is to find out who will use the system and then write for those users.

Documentation written for someone with a Ph.D. in engineering whose computer system will design and engineer parts and products will be quite different from documentation written for a clerk who is entering orders.

The prevalence of microcomputers in offices means that many users who are very knowledgeable about their own job responsibilities but have never seen a computer before are technically unsophisticated. Home users and small businesses often don't have technicians available to them. They must rely on the documentation so they can run their application systems. If the documentation is confusing or vague, users may give up in disgust or frustration. While some home users may find conquering a system a challenge, most will hate it. Small businesses, unlike home users, can't afford to spend a lot of time learning a system. Consequently, good documentation becomes more critical. Furthermore, even business users with an information center available for help don't want to have to call the information center personnel every time they try to do something new or run into a minor problem.

Determine the Users' Needs

Once you know who the users are, find out what they need to know about the system. The users' need for the system should have already been determined during the design of the system. You must determine what they need to know to use the system correctly and effectively.

To do that, it is helpful to know what they're doing now. Usually, a computer system does not represent a whole new function and a brand new set of output. It is usually a better way to do something already being done manually or with a different computer system. Therefore, by understanding the current procedures, you will know what has to change to do the same thing using the new system.

Talk to the Users

The best way to gather the information you need about users is to talk to them. Ask them what they need.

Make sure you talk to all the users. Often, for in-house business applications, you will be sent to the head of the user department. However, that person is probably not the only user. Clerks may be supplying the data. Secretaries may be completing the input forms. They are users just as those who use the reports are. You've already identified the users; talk to all of them.

When you interview users, include these questions:

How do you do this job now?

What forms do you use?

What information do you need?

What results do you get?

What reports do you produce?

How do you use these reports? Who sees them?

What is wrong with the way you're doing it now?

What do you expect the new system to do?

How will it make your job easier?

As you talk with the users, notice more than the answers to your questions. Look for non-verbal clues about how they feel about the new system.

Are they excited?

Are they apprehensive?

Do they know anything about computers?

Sometimes users are afraid that a new computer system will replace them. Their fear of losing their jobs may cause them to be apprehensive and uncooperative. You must be tactful and reassuring to get the information you want.

When a new system is online, users may be concerned about the security of their data. Then, you must reassure them, verbally and in the documentation, that the system's security measures prevent others from accessing their data.

Users of a new data base system may be very apprehensive about sharing data that formerly were theirs exclusively.

Thus, the writer often becomes a salesperson for the system. In interviews and in documentation, you may find it necessary to relieve apprehension by explaining the benefits of the system. For example, engineers may be reluctant to try computer graphics until they realize that they will benefit by reducing time and mistakes. Similarly, executives, whether they are in engineering companies or not, will become excited about computer graphics when they see business data in graphic representation created quickly and automatically. Users may also be apprehensive about the possibility of using computer terminals. They have heard about the hazards of radiation, eye problems, etc., that may result from using terminals. Then, the writer must understand ergonomics. You should reassure users about any ergonomic features in their equipment (grounding, anti-glare screens, tilt screens, etc.).

Let the users ask questions too. You can learn a great deal by the kinds of questions they ask. Build their confidence in you by finding the answers to questions you can't answer right away. This will make them more likely to cooperate with you now. Later, this confidence will help them to accept the system.

Unfortunately, some writers cannot interview their readers personally. If you write manuals for a software developer, or microcomputer users, or a time-sharing service, you probably will not have the opportunity for face-to-face conversations with users. In such cases, consider the questions any user might ask. Put yourself in the place of an inexperienced user. Use your knowledge of people in general.

When you don't know the users or their current situations, it is even more important that you understand the program thoroughly and that you write clearly.

Summary   Obtain background information about users through verbal and non-verbal communication.

Determine the Uses of the Documentation

Now that you know the users, imagine how they will use the documentation. If it is a manual:

Will they use it for reference? for training?

Will different people use different sections?

You don't want to write a manual that will sit on a shelf and collect dust. You have to know what the users will use.

See Chapter 4 for a further explanation about the kind of documentation to write.

Decide the Scope of the Documentation

User documentation can be very detailed or very simple. Determine how much detail users need. Usually, the more complex the application is, the more complex the documentation will be. For example, the documentation for a computer graphics system may present unique problems because the subject matter is more complex. The trick is to try to make even complicated applications as uncomplicated as possible via the user documentation.

The scope should be no broader than explaining the use of a specific system. Intricate details about the subject matter or about the system design belong somewhere else. You should never include more details than the users need. Extra verbiage will just make a manual too thick and overwhelming or make online documentation too expensive to store. If the documentation is too long, no one will want to read it.

On the other hand, users will find the documentation useless if it doesn't give them the detail they need. Your task is to use your knowledge of the user to determine the scope.

> Must you tell the users where to obtain input forms, or is that already known?

> Will the users of microcomputer packages understand the basic subject matter (word processing, spreadsheets, etc.), or should you explain it?

> Should you tell them how to distribute reports, where to file them, or how long to keep them; or do they already have procedures for this?

> Will the users be more comfortable if they know exactly what the computer does with their data, or will they accept the computer's accuracy as long as their reports are correct?

Ask yourself these and other questions and include only information that the users need.

Decide the Language of the Documentation

The users and their needs determine the kind of language you will use. Obviously, you would use different kinds of words if you were writing for executives with advanced degrees than you would if you were writing for clerical people who have recently completed high school. In Chapter 24, you will learn techniques for determining if the language you use is appropriate for the education and staff level of your readers.

The industry or application area also determines the appropriate language. Learn the language for that industry so you can write in terms the user will understand.

Avoid using data processing jargon for any user. However, some terms—*record, file, data base*—are unavoidable. Your knowledge of the user will determine if you should first define such terms before using them.

In summary, remember the following points when you obtain background information about the user.

Checklist for Obtaining User Information

1. Define *all* the users.

    a. Define how the user obtains and interfaces with the computer system.

    b. Define the user's industry and/or application.

    c. Define the user's level (organizational, educational, etc.).

2. Interview *all* the users.

3. Determine the use of the documentation.

4. Use the first 3 steps to decide the scope and language.

3

Compare Your Knowledge of the System and of the Users

When you understand the users and the system, you will know what the users need to know about the system and how that knowledge should be imparted in the documentation.

Determine What Parts of the Program the Users See

Your research from the programmers, the functional specifications, and the program specifications will give you a lot of detail that the users don't want to know. Most users don't care about files or job stream numbers. Sort out what information is visible to the users.

Microcomputer packages have more visible elements, since often the users are data entry operators, computer operators, data designers, and users all rolled into one. The users need to know the detail of how to make the calculations work and produce their output.

However, for large, in-house business systems on the company's mainframe, the users probably won't need every detail about the calculations, for example. A brief summary of calculations is all that is necessary in the instruction part of the documentation. If you feel that the users will have more confidence in the system if they know the formulas the computer uses, include the calculation formulas in an appendix. (See Chapter 16.) Calculation detail will only clutter the text.

Users who are not familiar with data processing operations and terminology won't care about or understand file descriptions or decision tables. If users need to know the implications of these, explain them in terms the users can understand.

Often, the actual data abbreviations used in the data dictionary are the names used only in the programs. The users will use an English word, not a program language word.

The program specifications are usually not important to the users. The users only care that the program does what it's supposed to do. As long as it works, the users probably won't care how.

Summary   Compare your knowledge of the system and of the user to determine how much to tell the user.

Make a List

Compare your notes about the system with your notes about the users. Make a list of the parts of the system the user needs to know about. For the Acme Distributing Company's purchase order/inventory system, the list might be like Example 3.1.

Example 3.1   List of Users/Documentation Sections

1. Management
   System overview
   Capabilities
   Reports

2. Order Clerks
   Input forms
   Data entry/update
   Error correction
   Reports

3. Sales Clerks
   Input forms
   Data entry/update
   Error correction
   Reports

4. Data Entry Department
   Input forms
   Data entry programs to use

> Keying procedures
> Procedures after keying
>
> 5. Set-Up/Operations
>   Preparation for processing
>   Processing/job streams
>   Output checking
>   Output handling

Each of these users sees different aspects of the system. Each of the users speaks a slightly different language. Computer room personnel have a jargon different from the clerical personnel, etc.

Whether you write for each user or for all the users, you must tell the users what they need to know in languages they can understand. When one manual or online set of instructions is for several users, different sections have different language levels. When this is impossible, use the simplest language level possible to insure understanding.

Frequently, such a list will not be necessary when writing for microcomputer users. These users are often the sole users of the system and perform all of the functions.

Review Your Knowledge

Part of this comparison process involves just sitting and thinking. Your mind really needs a break at this point to put things into focus. A photographer tries to find the right focus, angle, and perspective. That's what you have to do. Get the material into focus in your mind, decide the angle for approaching the material, and put it into the right perspective.

While you're thinking, new questions may arise. Go back to the users and programmers and talk to them. Tell them your perception; see if it's correct. This will help you discover information you may have missed and help you find the best way to say what you have to say.

Summary   Take time to decide exactly what parts of the system each type of user needs to understand.

Plan the User Documentation

The background information tells you what you must write. Next, you must plan the best way to present that material.

Now an architect would be ready to make blueprints. No architect would attempt to build anything without them. The result would be a hodge-podge. Similarly, you must have a blueprint or plan before you can write.

To plan you must decide what kind of user documentation to write (Chapter 4), organize the user documentation (Chapter 5), select the method of presentation (Chapter 6), determine the format and layout (Chapter 7), and use conventions and standards (Chapter 8).

4

Decide What Kind of User Documentation to Write

First, select the best medium (kind of documentation) for conveying specific information to a specific audience. Many options are available: audio cassettes, interactive online tutorials, printed manuals, etc. This book is primarily about written manuals. However, the same principles apply to writing the script for audio cassettes, the text for "help" screens, etc. Your purpose determines the medium. Of course, your purpose is to explain a system to its users. But that purpose is too broad. Narrow it.

> Is it an explanation to teach people how to use the system? (A training manual)
>
> Is it a reference to be used when the need arises? (A reference manual)
>
> Is it both of these? (A combination manual)
>
> Is it online user instruction?

You cannot write until your purpose is clearly defined.

The first three sections in this chapter are about printed manuals; the fourth is about online user documentation.

Is It a Training Manual?

If the manual's purpose is instruction, it is a training manual. Then, the manual can go from simple ideas to more complex ideas, building on the reader's growing comprehension. Introduce the users to the system and their responsibilities. Include guidelines for the typical flow of work.

Start with the assumption that the reader knows nothing about the system and explain it simply and logically. Remember the steps you followed to learn the system. The end result of a training manual is that readers, when they complete the manual, understand the system. You must have an objective for the instruction.

A good training manual is tutorial and should include ways to measure its success.

What will readers be able to do?

Under what conditions will they be able to do it?

How well must it be done?

The manual may include tests to answer these questions before the readers become actual users. The manual should be used in combination with training seminars.

Examples are important in any manual. They are vital in a training manual. Examples should explain each step and help motivate readers.

The training manual is a good place for conversion instructions. Conversion instructions explain how to convert from the old way of doing the tasks to the new system. Make the conversion instructions step-by-step procedures.

Is It a Reference Manual?

A reference manual differs from a training manual. A training manual teaches about the system. A reference manual is a collection of information organized so that specific information can be located as quickly and effortlessly as possible. It is not meant to be read from cover to cover. Only new employees are subjected to such tedium.

When writing a reference manual:

Organize topics to make them easy to find.

Explain deviations from the standard.

Be precise.

Leave nothing to chance.

Since you are not expecting anyone to read the manual from beginning to end, some information must be repeated wherever it is pertinent. You can never assume that the reader has read any other section; so each section must be complete in itself.

Is It a Combination Manual?

Most manuals for microcomputer packages will be combination manuals. Economics and practicality dictate that the manual first train the user and then provide an easy way to reference the material. A case study training session in the beginning of the manual followed by an alphabetic list of commands is an example of such a combination manual.

Ideally, large business systems have a training manual and a reference manual. However, since this is rarely the case, most manuals serve a dual purpose. Time constraints and policy may prevent you from writing two manuals for every system. Consider the possibility that you may write manuals that are both training and reference manuals. The first time the reader reads it all the way through for knowledge. After that, the reader uses it as a reference.

Such a manual must combine the objectives of training and reference manuals. Like a training manual, it must assume that the reader has no prior knowledge of the system. Like a reference manual, it must repeat information or instructions wherever they are pertinent. Since the organization cannot be strictly for reference, including an index becomes more important.

The advantage of this kind of manual is that system users will become familiar with the manual during a training seminar. Thus, they will be better equipped to use that manual when they are actually using the system.

Having a guide or manual for the person who will conduct a training seminar is important. It will help the seminar leader to pick those parts of the manual that are appropriate for training and to relate those to the parts of the manual that can be used for reference.

Is It Online User Documentation?

Online user documentation eliminates printed manuals. For users of online systems, it provides instructions on the terminals. The documentation is available online directly through the application system or as a stand-alone information retrieval system.

Traditionally, the most common form of online documentation is the help screen within an application. This concept requires writing skill to limit the help information and yet keep it effective. The maintenance of the help information is tied directly to program maintenance. Therefore, the writer must work closely with the programmers.

Other types of online documentation exist. Documentation processors combine word processing and data base technologies to produce an online "manual." This provides more detail than the traditional help screen approach. Through the touch of a key, it gives users immediate access to the most current information about the application system they are using. Producing this kind of online documentation normally requires documentation processor software.

The decision to use online user documentation is not usually the writer's alone. The use of help screens might involve company policy, the amount of disk storage available, the programmers, etc.

Online user documentation may require a separate training manual or online tutorial.

Summary   Define the purpose of the manual using your knowledge of the system and the users. Decide what kind of manual (or manuals) best suits the purpose.

5

Organize the User Documentation

Good organization will make the documentation's contents clear and accessible. The parts of the documentation must come together to help you communicate to your readers.

You've collected more information that you'll need. You've collected it from different sources. Now you've got to organize it. The order in which you collected the information is probably not the best way to organize it for your readers.

Before you can organize the material for your readers, you must first determine the kinds of organizational patterns that would be appropriate. Then you can decide which pattern best suits your needs and the users' needs. Then you can actually organize the documentation.

Determine the Kinds of Organization Possible

Even if you remember the classic organization patterns from your English classes, forget most of them. Cause and effect, contrast and comparison, inductive or deductive reasoning, etc., all are inappropriate organizational patterns for documentation writing.

Only a few options are open:

Order of importance   Put the most important ideas or items first. This may be appropriate for the introduction for a training manual or a reference manual.

Order of need   Put information first that the user is most likely to need most often. Use this in either training or reference manuals.

Order of difficulty   Start with the simpler concepts and go to more complex concepts. This is especially appropriate for a training manual.

Chronological   Begin with the first event or step. Use this for procedures.

Analytical   Divide a complex subject into its main parts and explain them. Use this for the overview or introduction.

Subject   Divide the manual by topics; for example, by system commands or by users' tasks. This may be appropriate for the input instructions or the output section.

Order of the Program   Organize the user documentation on the basis of the order in which the program will ask for information. This is appropriate for online systems and online user documentation.

One or all of these organizational patterns may be used. Organize based on your readers' needs. What is appropriate for one section or audience may be inappropriate for others.

Regardless of the organization method you choose, begin with a summary or overview at the beginning of each section. Documentation is not like a mystery novel; suspense is not appreciated in a manual. The subject of each section should be obvious from the beginning.

All effective writing begins with a summary that is informative and interesting. This gets the readers' interest and helps them understand the material. The summary must provide motivation. It should explain why the user would want to use the system or the function being described. The text that follows the overview will present points based on the opening overview. Without that overview, the reader may miss the significance of what follows.

In our case study, we may use a chronological/analytical organization for an introduction to the manual, as in Example 5.1.

The entire manual could be arranged by subject. Then, part of the table of contents would be like Example 5.2.

Another type of subject organization that has chronological order within each subject would be like Example 5.3.

Example 5.1   Introduction to the Documentation

A purchase order/inventory system consists of items being ordered, arriving, and being added to the inventory.

Items being ordered are represented by purchase orders. Purchase order information includes purchase order numbers, order date, supplier company, item quantity, and cost.

When the item arrives, we record the date received, the invoice number, and the check number of the check used to pay the invoice. The newly received item is compared with the purchase order information.

Inventory and its value increase by each item received. When we sell those items, inventory decreases and income increases.

Example 5.2   Table of Contents by Subject

Input Forms
   Purchase Order
   Merchandise Received
   Merchandise Sold

Reports
   Purchase Order Reports
   Inventory Reports

Example 5.3   Table of Contents by Subject, Chronological

Purchase Orders
   Input Form
   Data Entry
   Reports

Merchandise Received
   Input Form
   Data Entry
   Reports

Merchandise Sold
   Input Form
   Data Entry
   Reports

Example 5.4   Organization for Wonder-Calc

Basics of Wonder-Calc

Creating a spreadsheet

    Entering headings

    Entering numbers

    Editing and correcting headings and numbers

Saving the spreadsheet

Printing the spreadsheet

Ending the Wonder-Calc session

Wonder-Calc commands

    Copy

    Delete

    Insert

The organization of a microcomputer package's manual follows the same basic principles. Because you will not always know the chronological sequence in which the user intends to use the package, you can usually eliminate the chronological sequence method for these packages. Instead, use an organization that teaches the user how to use the system in a step-by-step way in the training part of the manual. In the reference part, use an organization that allows the user to find information quickly. For example, you might list commands and messages in alphabetic order. Example 5.4 illustrates an organization for a microcomputer manual.

Note that the first five main sections are in a step-by-step sequence that would be appropriate for learning the package. The last section lists the package's commands in alphabetic order.

Decide the Kind of Organization to Use

Consider the possible organizational patterns and decide which one (or combination) best suits the users' needs.

The important thing is that the material has some logical sequence. That logic must be transparent to the reader. The organization must place the correct emphasis on ideas or topics. The ideas that are presented first are often considered more important than those that are presented later.

The amount of detail given to a topic also affects the emphasis the reader perceives. A lot of detail signals importance.

Summary   Consider location and detail when you plan the manual's organization.

Develop a Preliminary Table of Contents

Some people call this an outline. But that's a dirty word to many people who think of Roman numerals, a B for every A, and parallel construction. This structured format has more to do with mechanics than writing. An outline is simply a device to organize your material. After all, isn't a table of contents really an outline without the Roman numerals? It puts everything you want to discuss into logical categories.

So forget the English class version of outlining and start categorizing all of the information you've gathered. Several easy ways to do this are available. Choose the one that best suits you.

Note cards

Lists

Diagrams

Note Cards   This method is flexible. You can arrange and rearrange until you're satisfied. Use 3 × 5 or 4 × 6 cards when you are obtaining the information. Or transfer relevant information to the cards. Put the cards into piles of related subjects. These piles will be based on the organization you've decided upon.

What about note cards that don't belong in any of the piles? Do they really belong in the manual? Eliminate anything that should not be included. It is impossible and inappropriate to include all the information you've gathered. Keep your readers in mind.

Each pile may be a chapter or main section of the manual.

Take the cards in each pile and sort them just as you did with all the cards in the first step. Then arrange the cards in an order that agrees with your organizational plan. Now you have the sub-headings.

Thus, the steps in using note cards to organize the material into a table of contents are:

1. Put all cards into piles by subject or topic.
2. Eliminate note cards that don't fit into subject categories.
3. Put the cards in each pile into smaller piles by sub-topics. (Repeat if necessary.)
4. Organize the sub-topic piles.
5. Arrange the subject piles (that are now in order by sub-topic) according to the organization plan.

Lists Make a list of everything you want to include. Forget about your organization plan for a minute. Just list everything! Number the items on your list.

Read over the list. What items seem to be related? How are they related? They probably belong in the same subject category. Make a list of those subject categories. Under each category, write the numbers from the list that identify the items that belong in that category. In our case study, part of the list might be like Example 5.5.

Example 5.5 List of Subjects for Table of Contents

1. Purchase order numbers = 8 digits
2. Inventory listed in alphabetic or item number order
3. Order clerks complete purchase order form
4. Quantity in inventory in 3rd column on report
5. Check number supplied by Accounting Department
6. Supplier company description cannot be more than 30 characters
7. Purchase order number pre-stamped on input form

Example 5.6   Using the List of Subjects

```
Purchase Orders
1
3
6
7
```

One subject category would be Purchase Orders. Under that heading, we would write the numbers referring to purchase orders. As with the note cards, eliminate any non-pertinent information. Sub-divide as much as appropriate.

The steps in using lists to organize the material into a table of contents are:

1. List all the items you want to include.

2. Determine which items are related by subject.

3. List those subjects.

4. Write the numbers of the items that pertain to that subject.

Diagrams   Sometimes a picture is an easy way to visualize the organization. A system flowchart usually contains information that the user doesn't need or want. But a simple box diagram can be developed into a table of contents, especially if the organization is chronological.

In our case study, a diagram for the purchase order entry portion might be like Example 5.7. In this diagram, rectangles mean an action to be taken by the user. Diamonds represent a decision; the user must decide whether to answer the question "yes" or "no." From this diagram, the section of a table of contents shown in Example 5.8 develops.

Regardless of the method you use, developing a table of contents gets your ideas and your organization down on paper in a formatted way. When those ideas and plans are a hodge-podge of notes or just in your head, you don't have a blueprint. But when they're down on paper, you do. Any flaws in logic or organization or any gaps in information should become apparent.

For the preliminary table of contents, write headings that are

Example 5.7   Diagram for Table of Contents

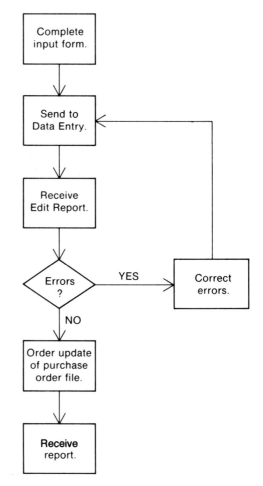

Example 5.8   Using the Diagram

Purchase Order Processing
    Input Form Completion Procedures
    Data Entry Procedures
    Error Correction Procedures
    Report Interpretation

meaningful and as specific as possible. Make sure all the sub-headings relate to the heading and that the heading spans all of its sub-headings. Use parallel phrasing for parallel ideas. This means that ideas of equal value should be expressed in the same grammatical form.

Notice that in the preceding example all of the sub-headings refer to the main heading, Purchase Order Processing. All of the sub-headings have the same grammatical structure: the last words in the sub-headings are all nouns, and the words that precede the nouns describe the nouns. The sub-headings are in a logical sequence, chronological order.

Once you've written the preliminary table of contents, half the task is over. Now you can determine how much you have to write and how long it will take you to write it. Thus, you can budget your time more accurately. You've done yourself a favor by getting organized. And you've done the readers a favor by giving them a thorough, logical table of contents.

Of course, the final table of contents for the manual will have to wait until the manual is written. It is the last part of the manual to be finalized. The manual's table of contents will have page numbers. Obviously, these won't be available until the manual is in its final form. Some headings and sub-headings may change as you write. But a preliminary, working table of contents is essential before you write.

Checklist for Organizing the Documentation

1. Determine every idea or topic you want to include in the manual.
2. Put all those ideas or topics into main categories.
3. Subdivide the main categories.
4. Decide on a logical sequence for presenting the ideas or topics.
5. Write a preliminary table of contents.

6

Select the Method of Presentation

Besides knowing what you want to present and the order in which to present it, you must decide *how* to present it. The way the material appears on the page affects the reader. So decide which method best suits your reader and your material.

Five methods of presentation are appropriate for documentation:

1. Prose
2. Cookbook style
3. Numbered instructions
4. Playscript style
5. Four-step method

A manual may use any or all of these methods. Regardless of which method of presentation you choose, always include figures that illustrate what the text is saying. Chapters 20 and 21 go into greater detail about figures and illustrations.

Use Prose

Prose, in the context of writing documentation, means using paragraphs. It is the ordinary form of most writing. It is straight text. An example of a prose presentation for the purchase order/inventory system is Example 6.1.

Example 6.1   Instructions in Prose Style

> Order clerks complete the Purchase Order Input Form (form number PO123). The form has a preprinted purchase order number. The clerk enters the date, supplier company name, the item, the quantity, and the cost.
>
> The clerks send the form to the Data Entry Department where the information is keyed to an input tape. The tape goes to the computer and updates the purchase order file.

Notice that this method causes some of the information to be lost in the paragraphs. Compare this with the example in the next section.

Use Cookbook Style

Cookbook style, as its name implies, means the instructions are written like a recipe:

> Beat until smooth.
> Bake at 350° for 1 hour.

The verb is the first word in the sentence. This allows you to state the instructions in fewer words than in the straight text of the prose presentation.

Example 6.2 gives the same instructions as the prose example but uses cookbook style. It has about twenty fewer words and says essentially the same thing. Shorter reading lines mean faster reading and quicker understanding.

Example 6.2   Instructions in Cookbook Style

> Complete the Purchase Order Input Form, PO123.
>
> Enter the date, supplier company name, item, quantity, and cost.

> Send the form to Data Entry.
>
> Key the data to a tape.
>
> Process the tape on the computer.
>
> Update the purchase order file.

Summary   Whenever you are giving instructions, use some form of the cookbook style of presentation. Put the verb first. If the instruction has a condition, state the condition; then follow it immediately with the verb.

Use Numbered Instructions

Numbering the steps or procedures is often more appropriate in documentation writing than prose and has its basis in the cookbook style.

Example 6.3 gives the same instructions as the previous examples. The numbered instructions follow the order of the input form. The capitalized words are headings from the input form.

Example 6.3   Numbered Instructions

> Order clerks complete the Purchase Order Input Form (PO123).
>
>   1. PURCHASE ORDER NUMBER   The number is preprinted on the form.
>   2. DATE   Enter the current date. Use 6 digits; the 2-digit month, the 2-digit day, and the last 2 digits of the year. For example, October 25, 1982 is 102582.
>   3. SUPPLIER COMPANY   Enter the name of the company that will receive the order. Use up to 30 characters.
>   4. ITEM NO.   Enter the item number of the item being ordered. Find the item number on the inventory list-

ing. If this is a new item, see the Adding New Items section.

5. QUANTITY   Enter the quantity being ordered. Use up to 99999.

6. COST/ITEM   Enter the cost of each item. Use up to $9999.99. (The system will calculate the total cost of this order.)

7. PREPARED BY   Sign your name.

8. Send the completed form to the Data Entry Department.

9. Data Entry personnel will key the data and submit the resulting data tape to computer operations personnel.

10. Operations personnel will process the tape so that the data update the purchase order file.

Note that this method of presentation makes clear exactly what has to be done. A paragraph would be quite cluttered if it contained all of the information about data length.

This method takes up a little more space, but it reads more quickly. It also makes it easier for the readers to find exactly what they need.

Use Playscript Style

The fourth method is helpful when the instructions are addressed to more than one group of users. As its name implies, it is written like the script of a play. It names the actor, then the action. It also is based on the cookbook style.

Example 6.4   Instructions in Playscript Style

ORDER CLERK	1. Complete the Purchase Order Input Form (PO123).
	a. PURCHASE ORDER NUMBER The number is preprinted on the form.
	b. DATE Enter the current date. Use 6 digits; the 2-digit month, the 2-digit day, and the last 2 digits of the year. For example, August 6, 1982 is 080682.
	c. SUPPLIER COMPANY Enter the name of the company that will receive the order. Use up to 30 characters.
	d. ITEM NO. Enter the item number of the item being ordered. Find the item number of the inventory listing. If this is a new item, see the Adding New Items section.
	e. QUANTITY Enter the quantity being ordered. Use up to 99999.
	f. COST/ITEM Enter the cost of each item. Use up to $9999.99. (The system will calculate the total cost of this order.)
	g. PREPARED BY Sign your name.
	2. Send the form to Data Entry.
DATA ENTRY PERSONNEL	3. Key the data from form PO123.
	4. Give resulting tape to Operations.
OPERATOR	5. Process the tape to update the purchase order file.

This method takes up more room than the numbered instructions. Obviously, a lot of space on the page is lost. But your goal isn't saving paper; it's making instructions clear and easy to understand.

The prose method submerged all the instructions in text. The numbered instructions method still submerged the doer, the actor.

The playscript method makes the doer clear. Different users need read only the instructions that apply to them. Use the playscript method whenever there are multiple users for the same section of the manual.

Use the Four-Step Method

In some more flexible systems, the user has more latitude of action than in the examples above. This is especially true for microcomputer packages and software developed for third-party use. The playscript method will not work, for example. Even if more than one user could use the package, you will not know who will be doing what. One step does not necessarily follow another. Instead, the user must decide what to do and when to do it. If this is the case, only the prose method or the four-step method will work. The manual must provide guidance about when and why to do functions.

Four steps will provide this guidance:

1. Motivation or reasons. What do the users want to do? Why do they want to do it?
2. Effect. What will happen when users do this?
3. General steps. What are the typical steps to accomplish the desired effect?
4. Example.

Example 6.5   Instructions Using the Four Step Method

Wonder-Calc Print Command

Use the Print command to get a paper copy of your spreadsheet. Wonder-Calc will print as many columns across the page as will fit on your paper. You can change Wonder-Calc's margins by specifying the top and bottom margins and the print length and width. After you get the paper copy of your spreadsheet, you can cut and paste the printed pages to form the total spreadsheet.

The general steps for printing your spreadsheet are

1. Make sure the printer is connected properly, turned on, and loaded with paper.

2. Press *P.*

3. If the margins pre-set by Wonder-Calc are acceptable, press [RETURN]. Your spreadsheet will begin printing.

4. If you wish to change the margins, press *M* for the Margin sub-command. The screen displays the margins that Wonder-Calc has pre-set. Use the [TAB] key to move the cursor to the margins you want to change. Enter the new margins. Press [RETURN].

5. After completing step 4, you are still in the Print command. Press [RETURN] to begin printing the spreadsheet.

For example, Wonder-Calc's pre-set margins display when you press *M* within the Print command:

MARGINS: Left: 6   Top: 8   Width: 72
          Length: 60   Paper Size: 66

You can change these margins depending on the size of your paper and your spreadsheet:

MARGINS: Left: 12   Top: 3   Width: 60
          Length: 60   Paper Size: 66

See Chapter 14, Example 14.2, for another example of writing procedures when the user has to decide what to do and why.

Use Combinations

Different methods of presentation can be appropriate for different manuals and different sections of the same manual.

Use prose for the overview or introduction. Use cookbook style or numbered instructions in sections that address only one user. Use playscript style for sections that have more than one user.

Further References

Mathees, Leslie H. *The New Playscript Procedures.* Stamford, Connecticut: Office Publications Inc., 1977.

Use this book for further reference on writing manuals using the playscript method.

The Manuals Corporation of America (MCA) (53 William Penn Drive, Stony Brook, New York, 11790) conducts seminars and provides material that can help with methods of presentation, especially with playscript style.

7

Determine the Format and Layout

The physical appearance of the manual's page is important. Visual simplicity helps the reader. If the manual looks confusing, the readers will have negative impressions before they even begin to read. Format and layout define the arrangement of information on the page and make reading easier.

Even the color of the paper and ink used can make a manual more pleasing visually. Different manuals for the same company can have different colored paper and covers so users can tell them apart easily. Manual writers must do everything they can to make manuals as easy to read as possible.

Therefore, you must develop a format and layout to use for the entire manual.

Define the Format

Format is a set arrangement for information that is on every page of the manual. Such information may include:

Title

Section

Page number

Date

Update information

All of these items should appear in the same place on every page. That way the readers know where to find the page number or section heading when they are looking for something.

Example 7.1   Blank Stationery

PURCHASE ORDER/INVENTORY USER'S GUIDE	SECTION: PAGE: DATE: UPDATED:

Microcomputer manuals can vary greatly in their format. However, in-house installations often have strict, consistent format.

If you use special paper or stationery for manuals, format is determined automatically. For our case study, blank stationery could be preprinted as in Example 7.1. If you don't have manuals stationery, decide on a consistent placement for the constant information.

An exception to consistent placement may be page numbers. It may be easier for users if page numbers are on an outside corner. That means, when the manual uses two-sided pages, they'll be on the right side of the page for right-hand pages and on the left side for left-hand pages. Thus, for two-sided pages, the format for right- and left-hand pages may be the mirror image of one another.

Page numbers must have a format of their own. You've probably seen page numbers that take up half a line on the page. Such very long page numbers contain several kinds of information—a section number, a page number, a revision number, etc. These numbering systems are flexible, and many manual writers use them. But the reader rarely needs all that information. Anyway, the writer is probably the only one who knows how to extract all the information from the number.

The purpose of a page number is to allow readers to find a specific topic on a specific page. The reader finds the topic in the table of contents or index, notes the page number, and turns to that page. It is easier to remember page 86 than page II–11–10–2.5. It is easier for a conference leader using a training manual to say, "Turn to page 37," than it is to say, "Turn to page III–12–29–34.2."

If a manual has numbered section dividers, it may be appropriate to renumber for each section. The section number would precede the page number.

Of course, manuals may require updating. An update that is longer than what it replaces can destroy the page numbering scheme. In such cases, add a decimal point and a number.

Thus, the best format for page numbering is

1, 2, 3, . . . , 25.

If page 25 is replaced by an addition that is 3 pages long, the page numbers are

25, 25.1, 25.2.

Define the Layout

Layout is the arrangement of all the rest of the information not covered by format, information that will not appear on every page. Layout includes paper size and margin width. A typical page might be 8½ by 11 inches with a 1¼-inch right margin, a 1½-inch left margin, and 1-inch top and bottom margins. (Left margins must be wider to allow for binding or drilled holes.)

The layout determines whether text is single- or double-spaced and how many spaces appear between paragraphs and sub-headings. When you define the layout, call for extra blank lines in between headings. That extra white space is visually pleasing, and it makes topics easier to find. Use headings whenever the subject changes. But don't use too many. You don't want the manual to look like an outline.

Headings help you write and the readers read. With headings, you don't have to worry so much about topic sentences and transitions. The readers can find subjects and have places to stop. (Remember, however, that readers sometimes ignore headings. Don't overlook the importance of topic sentences.)

Thus, your layout must provide not only for placement of headings but for different levels of headings. Chapter titles could be in all CAPITAL letters. Headings within the chapter could be in Upper and Lower Case Letters underlined.

Consider other ways to make headings stand out. Centering them is often effective. If the capability is available to you, change the size of the type or use bold typefaces. Even if you do not have

Example 7.2   Layout without Headings

Chapter 1   SYSTEM OVERVIEW

The purchase order/inventory system keeps track of items from the time they are ordered until they are sold. The system maintains information for items being ordered, arriving, increasing inventory, and decreasing inventory.

The first step is the purchase order. Purchase order information includes purchase order number, order date, supplier company, item, quantity, and cost. Order clerks prepare these data, and they increase the purchase order file.

When the ordered items arrive, they increase inventory. Clerks supply information including item, quantity, and date to the computer.

a typesetter, you can use typewriters with larger typefaces or press-type (letters that rub off the sheet onto the page). If available, lettering machines or press-type makes headings more effective than simply capitalizing and underlining.

Compare the two layouts in Examples 7.2 and 7.3. Both have the same words for an overview to our purchase order/inventory system. But they have totally different layouts. The second one uses more headings and white space. It is easier to read because of the breaks.

Some sections of the manual may require special layouts. For example, the input form instructions will be easier to understand if an input form sample is on the left-hand page and the instructions

Example 7.3   Layout with Headings

Chapter 1   SYSTEM OVERVIEW

Purpose

The purchase order/inventory system keeps track of items from the time they are ordered until they are sold. The system maintains information for items being ordered, arriving, increasing inventory, and decreasing inventory.

> Purchase Orders
>
> The first step is the purchase order. Purchase order information includes purchase order number, order date, supplier company, item, quantity, and cost. Order clerks prepare this data, and it increases the purchase order file.
>
> Inventory
>
> When the ordered items arrive, they increase inventory. Clerks supply information including item, quantity, and date to the computer.

on the right. See Chapter 13, Write the Input Instructions, for an example of this.

For online systems that use commands, the layout should include an example of each command from beginning to end. Thus, the layout would be an explanation of the purpose and procedures for a command followed by a computer-printed sample of that command. See Chapter 14, Write the Operating Instructions, for an example of this.

Summary   Format and layout help reader interpret, comprehend, and remember the material.

Further Reference

The Manuals Corporation of America (MCA) (53 William Penn Drive, Stony Brook, New York, 11790) conducts seminars and provides material that can help with format and layout.

8

Use Conventions
and Standards

Conventions are standard methods for presenting similar material within a manual. Standards are guidelines that help plan, organize, and write the manual.

Use Conventions

As you plan the manual, you will realize that several situations are common to much of the material. Reading will be easier and quicker if every similar situation has a similar presentation. Such similar presentations are called conventions. Conventions provide fixed usage, clarify the meaning, and shorten the text.

Normally, conventions are few in a microcomputer manual, since the systems often involve unstructured user interaction. However, conventions apply easily to batch and online systems.

Determine When Conventions Are Appropriate Conventions are appropriate in many situations. The three situations here will give you an idea of the kind of situations that are appropriate for conventions.

Variable material

User-entered material

Terminal key reference

Often what the user can enter into a system can be almost anything as long as it is the correct length. In such cases, a conventional way to represent that *variable material* is helpful. For example, use lowercase n's to represent numeric variable material. Example 8.1 means, "enter any number, using up to 4 digits," but it's much shorter.

Example 8.1   Numeric Variable Material

Enter nnnn.

Lowercase x's can represent alphabetic or numeric variable material. Example 8.2 means, "enter any 4 characters you choose."

Example 8.2   Alphabetic or Numeric Variable Material

Enter xxxxx.

Sometimes part of the information must be a certain way and the rest is variable. Example 8.3 means, "the inventory file must begin with INV, followed by any 3 numbers."

Example 8.3   Partly Variable Material

Name the inventory file INVnnn.

When you explain *user-entered material,* sometimes you'll explain the *kind* of information to enter, as in Example 8.4. Other times, you'll tell the user *exactly* what to enter, as in Example 8.5.

Example 8.4   General Instructions

Enter the supplier company name.

Example 8.5   Exact Instructions

> Enter "WID" for widgets.

However, a convention that says user-entered data are capitalized and underlined or in boldface type or italics helps reading. It makes user-entered data stand out in the text. It looks less cluttered than using quotation marks. Sometimes quotation marks could be part of an entry; underlining, boldface, or italics never is.

Example 8.6   Using Italics or Boldface

> Enter *WID* for widgets.
> Enter **WID** for widgets.

Online systems lend themselves to *terminal key references*. Users sit at computer terminals and press keys. Often every entry must be followed by pressing a certain key.

It is helpful to have a conventional way to designate keys on the terminal keyboard. One good way is to bracket the names of the keys. For example, [RETURN] means the carriage return key.

Different manufacturers of terminals call keys by different names. The carriage return key may be marked "Return" or "CR" or something else. If your manual is for in-house users, all the terminals will probably be from the same manufacturer. Refer to keys by whatever abbreviations are on the keys themselves. However, when your manual is for users outside your own organization, they probably will have different terminals. If you know the users, find out what kind of terminals they have. Find out the most common key names. If you don't know your users, use the key names most common in the industry.

If you use a convention for keys, notice how much easier writing the manual becomes. The first part of Example 8.7 doesn't use a convention; the second part does.

Example 8.7   Instructions without or with a Convention

> Enter *WID* for widgets. Press the key marked "Return" on the
> terminal keyboard.
>
> Enter *WID* for widgets. [RETURN]

The second sentence in the part without the convention would be
repeated for every instruction! The one word is much easier. Better
yet, have a convention that "every entry ends with [RETURN]."

Decide How to Use Conventions   These are only some ways conventions can help you and your reader. Your system and its users
determine what conventions will be good for your manual.

Conventions should be simple and easy to understand. If the
users don't know what the conventions are or what they mean,
conventions defeat their own purpose. So don't have too many conventions and keep them simple.

Summary   If conventions will help user understanding, develop
them and use them consistently.

Use Standards

Writing user manuals should be governed by standards. Standards
are written guidelines that define the content, approach, and objectives of the manual. They provide procedures and guidelines for
all aspects of user manuals: writing, reviewing, printing, and updating. Standards will provide a plan for other, similar manuals.

Standards should not be rigid rules but flexible guidelines. Every
computer system has its own characteristics that make parts of
the manual unique. The guidance offered by standards makes the
writing process easier and promotes consistency when consistency
is possible.

Include All Aspects   Standards should include every aspect that
is common to all user manuals. Develop standards for:

Scope (See Chapter 4)

Organization (See Chapter 5)

Method of presentation (See Chapter 6) This may differ for different systems, but standards offer guidelines.

Format (See Chapter 7)

Layout (Headings) (See Chapter 7)

Page numbering (See Chapter 7)

Conventions (See Chapter 8)

Style (See Section 3)

Graphics (See Chapters 18 and 19)

Review procedures (See Chapter 23)

Form (See Chapter 25)

Updating (See Section 10)

Responsibilities

Note that all but one of these areas requiring standards are covered in other chapters. You must determine the approach that best suits you, your users, and the system. Then, standardize that approach.

Responsibilities (other than review responsibilities), however, are not covered elsewhere in this book. Yet standards that spell out who is responsible for every aspect of the manual are important.

Provide a Uniform Plan Standards provide a uniform plan for handling every aspect of the user manual. They also make writing faster because you need not plan each detail every time you write another manual. Instead, you can use the time to decide how to approach what is unique to the system.

Standards also help the users. Often, in-house users are exposed to more than one computer system. If the organization, page numbering scheme, conventions, etc., are as similar as possible for all your manuals, users won't waste time trying to find information. They'll already know how to use the manual. They'll learn to expect where to find certain kinds of information.

Summary Standards help everyone involved in developing the manual. Everyone is more comfortable when there are no surprises.

PART II

When You Write

After all your research and planning, you are ready to write. The outline (the preliminary table of contents) and the decisions about the kind of manual and method of presentation tell you *what* to write. This part of the book will tell you *how* to write it. The way you write will be the same, whether the user documentation is online or printed in a manual.

Don't start too soon. If you're still not sure about the plan or the information, go back and clear up any questions. You can't write clearly until everything is clear in your mind.

However, avoiding writing too early does *not* mean you must wait until all the programming is done. From your research, you know what the system should do. Trust the programmers to make the system do just that. Write while they are programming. Then, the manual and the system will be done at approximately the same time. Too often, computer personnel and users complain that they have to wait to use a new system because the manual isn't ready. Proper timing will eliminate this complaint.

Of course, we are assuming an ideal situation—that the system and manual are being developed at the same time. If this is not the case, write as soon as you've completed your research and planning.

This part explains how to adapt writing skills to writing manuals. For help with basic writing skills refer to the references listed at the ends of Chapters 9, 10, and 11.

When you write, you should use the right style (Section 3) to write each section of the documentation (Section 4). In manuals, use examples, diagrams, and illustrations (Section 5) to enhance the reader's understanding. After these steps, you are ready to type the manual (Section 6).

Use the Right Style

To write well, you must be able to get your ideas across simply and clearly. This section of the book will help you do that. Style is the way words are put together to form phrases and sentences. It includes word choice, usage, and punctuation.

The style advocated here is using short words and sentences. Big words, long sentences, and a heavy style are not the way to get your ideas across. People often write with that heavy, academic style because they think they're supposed to. But such a style won't lead to understanding. And what cannot be understood is often overlooked. Users' understanding of the system is the primary purpose of the manual.

Therefore, forget the style you were taught in English class. It probably stressed big words, vocabulary prowess, and fancy sentence structures. Instead, use simple words and simple sentences.

The right style for manuals means using clear, simple words (Chapter 9), active voice verbs (Chapter 10), and effective punctuation (Chapter 11).

9

Use Simple, Clear Language

Mark Twain once wrote in a letter, "I notice you use plain, simple language, short words, and brief sentences. That is the way to write English." How true! It is even more true when you are writing manuals. Correct word choice is essential to user understanding. The words you write must mean the same thing to everyone who reads them.

That also means, be explicit. For example, if you want the user of a terminal to press the key marked "enter," say so. Don't write, "Type an enter." The user just may type, "AN ENTER."

Usually, words that lead to understanding are simple, everyday words. The following list has big words we often use that can be replaced with simpler, shorter, clearer words.

Why Say:	When You Can Say:
utilize	use
terminate	end
initiate	start, begin
numerous	many
modify	change

The list could go on and on, but you get the idea. If a short word can replace a long word, use it.

Another habit many writers get into is changing verbs to nouns. For example, these nouns take unnecessarily long verbs and add "tion":

Noun	Verb	Shorter Verb or Noun
utilization	utilize	use
modification	modify	change
termination	terminate	end

They are weak words because they hide or disguise the verb.

Of course, sometimes you must use big words. "Inventory," for example, is a fairly long word. But it's the only one that means exactly what it does. Therefore, you should certainly use it. The idea is to use words no more complicated than necessary.

Just as you should avoid long words, you should also avoid long-winded expressions. We use windy expressions all the time. But the following list shows that it's not necessary.

Why Say:	When You Can Say:
at the present time	now
maximum quantity	most
minimum quantity	least
a large portion of	many
a major portion of	most
in order that	so
due to the fact that	since

Like the other lists, this one could go on and on. The point is, use the fewest and shortest words possible. This advice helps the users read faster. No one wants to dwell over each page of a manual as you might with a novel. The users want to read fast to figure out what they're supposed to do. Even if you feel some beautifully written passage is dramatic or inspired, forget it.

A few hints will help you choose the best words.

Conversational style

Consistent words

Correct, consistent capitalization

Careful abbreviations

No computer jargon

Let's explore what these mean.

Use a Conversational Style

You don't have to change your vocabulary as soon as you put something on paper. Write the way you talk. Look back at the lists of shorter words and phrases. Wouldn't you almost always use the words in the right columns if you were talking instead of writing? Don't we usually talk in short sentences? Don't we get annoyed when people flaunt their big vocabularies or try to impress us with technical jargon? Well, writing shouldn't be any different.

Obviously, writing the way you talk doesn't mean forgetting correct grammar. We can get away with sentence fragments and incorrect noun/verb agreement when we talk but not when we write. No one talks with visible punctuation marks. If our writing is to be understood, though, we must write with correct punctuation.

The writer doesn't have the chance to stop and explain the way a speaker does. Nor does the writer have the advantage of voice inflection. The meaning must come from the words themselves and the way they are arranged in sentences and paragraphs.

Summary   Write the way you talk but more carefully.

The following suggestions may help you write with a conversational style that is a little more precise than conversation.

Use contractions.

Ask questions.

Talk to the reader.

Use short sentences.

Eliminate "which" and "that."

Avoid slang.

Don't avoid clichés and idioms.

Use Contractions   We have all heard at one time or another that formal writing shouldn't include contractions. Yet, we all use contractions when we speak. They're perfectly good, grammatically correct words. They make the sentences flow better. The only time contractions are inappropriate is when you want to emphasize a point. Somehow, "We won't update the file more than once a week"

Example 9.1   Talking to the Reader

> After the user receives the report, he or she should check it.
>
> After you receive the report, check it.

just doesn't have the emphatic quality of, "We will not update the file more than once a week."

Ask Questions   Questions are a natural part of conversation. Use them, when appropriate, in your writing. Ask the same questions the users might ask; then answer them. Don't overdo this technique, however. It can lose its effect.

Talk to the Reader   In this "conversation," you are talking to the reader. The reader *is* the user. Therefore, don't call the reader "the user." Call the reader "you." Address your writing to the reader as if you were engaged in conversation. Besides being more personal, calling the reader "you" helps avoid a sticky problem for writers—sexist personal pronouns. In Example 9.1, the first sentence calls the reader the "user." The second sentence calls the reader "you." "You" is unisex. It avoids the "he or she," "he/she" controversy.

Use Short Sentences   Short sentences are easier to read, write, and punctuate than long ones. Each sentence should have only one idea. That way you won't lose any important ideas. Studies show that 15 to 20 words per sentence make sentences easy to read. Don't, however, make every sentence exactly the same length. The reader may fall asleep! As a general rule, make each sentence as simple as it possibly can be and still convey the meaning. Short sentences usually have only one punctuation mark, a period. Remember, punctuation rules for periods are a lot easier to deal with than rules for commas, semicolons, and colons.

Eliminate "Which" and "That"   Those two words signal a long sentence coming. Your goal is short sentences. "Which" or "that" usually signals another idea. Thus, the other idea should be another

Example 9.2   Eliminating "Which" and "That"

Error messages that explain which data are incorrect help the user.

Error messages explaining incorrect data help the user.

sentence. For example, the first sentence in Example 9.2 is confusing. "That" and "which" are not necessary. The second sentence is much better.

Avoid Slang   Slang, although prevalent in conversation, has no place in a manual.

Don't Avoid Clichés and Idioms   Sometimes the old, time-worn phrases are the clearest way to get exactly what you mean across to the reader.

Use Consistent Language

Now that we've seen that the shortest word for something is usually the best word, stick to it. Don't look for synonyms. Your purpose is to inform and instruct, not to offer vocabulary variety.

Don't call something a "command" one time, a "function" another time, and an "instruction" a third time. The reader may think you mean three different things.

Inconsistent word usage that can be understood still can be annoying. For example, you can do many things on a terminal keyboard. You can hit, press, tap, strike, type, and depress the keys to enter, type, or input the data. Decide that users should *press* the keys to *enter* data (or whatever combination you prefer), and use those words throughout the manual.

The same words in inconsistent form can also be confusing or annoying. Is filename different from file name? A database from a data base? Online from on-line or on line?

What is the manual called? A user's guide? A users' guide? A user guide? A user manual? User procedures? Decide on a title and always call it, and all similar documents, by that title. Put the system name in front of the consistent title. For our case study we could use Purchase Order/Inventory System User's Guide.

Summary   Consistent word usage helps you write and helps the user understand.

Use Correct, Consistent Capitalization

Consistent capitalization is important too. If command names are going to be all capital letters, they should always appear that way. Don't write, "the ENTER command" in one place and "the Enter command" in another. Don't write, "the ENTER and the Change commands."

If you capitalize the name of the system, do so consistently. If it's the Purchase Order/Inventory System, never write "the Purchase order/inventory system" or "the purchase order/inventory system."

Use Abbreviations Cautiously

Abbreviations and acronyms can be aggravating to the reader. Acronyms are words formed with the first letter or first few letters of several words. Computer terminology is full of acronyms. Computer technicians tend to talk in acronyms. It's not uncommon to hear sentences such as, "We're going from OS to DOS." Or, "Our JCL uses a PROCLIB." *Never use these in a manual without explanation.* Sometimes users must deal with JCL (job control language) or DOS (direct operating system). They must learn the terms and use them. However, include only the terms that users must know. If you include unnecessary technical terms, your readers will put the manual on the shelf to collect dust.

Only use abbreviations that relate to the user's vocabulary and subject area. For example, purchase order is often abbreviated to PO. Even then always explain the abbreviation the first time you use it. For example, your first reference might be "a purchase order (PO). . . ." Subsequent uses could be "PO."

Never assume that your readers will know what abbreviations mean. Maybe you think that everyone knows that "A/R" means "accounts receivable." Even so, explain it at least once.

The abbreviations for "for example" (e.g.) and "that is" (i.e.) are often abused or used incorrectly. The abbreviations are from Latin, and Latin scholars are rare these days. Thus, it's easy to switch the two. Rather than risk using the wrong one or confusing the reader, use "for example" and "that is" rather than their Latin abbreviations. Another Latin abbreviation is "etc." It means "and so forth." It's often useful when it's impossible to cover every alternative. Just remember, it's "etc." not "ect." Don't use "etc." very often. After all, Latin cannot be classified as clear, simple language to English-speaking readers.

Avoid Computer Jargon

Besides computer acronyms, other jargon is also widespread. If you're a technician or have worked with technicians, you know that bits, bytes, files, records, and other terms are part of everyday conversation in a computer center. But, even though computer use and familiarity are growing, those words still may not be part of the everyday conversation of users. Often these words are the best words to describe a concept. (New concepts need new words.) Then, use the computer word; it is worth the effort to explain it. Therefore, explain every computer term you must use. Define the following:

Record

Data

File

Master file

Data base

Disk

Tape

Default

Again, the list is incomplete. Explain items when you use them, or in a glossary, or in both places. The idea is, if it's related to computers and you must use it, explain it. (See the Glossary at the end of this book.)

It will probably be necessary for users to talk to computer personnel. They must be able to communicate. Some computer terms will have to be part of that communication.

Users don't want to read about subroutines, program numbers, or main memory address space. Users care about the part of the program that is visible to them. Ordinarily, they are not concerned about the inner workings of a system. Knowing that about users can eliminate a lot of the computer jargon in the manual. It may never be necessary to explain that the data are stored on a disk and accessed via CICS (Customer Information Control System from IBM). However, assure users that stored data will not get lost. Online systems often have commands for saving data. Explain to users when and how to save their data.

Summary   The style for manuals uses words that are clear and simple to the user. Short words and short sentences improve reading and understanding. Don't explain too much. What you must explain, explain in the user's language.

Further References

Brogan, John A. *Clear Technical Writing.* New York: McGraw-Hill Book Company, 1973.
Chapters 1, 2, 3, 8, 9, 10, and 11 contain exercises that will help you use clear, simple words.

Joseph, Albert. *Put It in Writing.* Cleveland, Ohio: The International Writing Institute, Inc., 1979.
This book offers many suggestions for clear writing and expands upon the ideas presented in this book. Mr. Joseph focuses on business writing and has written and conducted writing seminars for many companies.

The Manuals Corporation of America (MCA) (53 William Penn Drive, Stony Brook, New York, 11790) conducts seminars that will help you write with clear words and short sentences.

Writing without Bias. San Francisco: International Association of Business Communicators, 1977.

10

Use Active Voice Verbs

"Voice" in grammar means the relationship between the subject and the verb. Active voice is the grammarian's term to mean that the subject of the sentence does the acting. The opposite is the passive voice, in which the subject of the sentence is acted upon.

Example 10.1   Active and Passive Voice

> Active voice: The clerk completes the input form.
>
> Passive voice: The input form was completed by the clerk.

In the active sentence, "clerk" is the subject and is doing the action described by the verb. In the passive sentence, "form" is the subject and is not doing anything; something is being done to it. It *receives* the action of the verb.

To make this a little clearer, let's review a very basic English class teaching. The most common sentence structure in written English is that shown in Example 10.2.

Example 10.2   Active Voice Structure

Subject	Verb	Direct Object
Clerk	completes	form.

That basic structure demands the active voice. Learn to differentiate between active and passive voice verbs.

Recognize Active and Passive Voice Verbs

The difference between the two voices may seem academic to some. Therefore, learn some simple ways to recognize each. The easiest way to recognize passive and active voice verbs is to follow these steps:

1. Find the subject of the sentence.
2. Find the action (verb) in the sentence.
3. Is the subject performing the action?
   "Yes" means the verb is active.
   "No" means the verb is passive.

Passive voice verbs almost always have some form of the verb "to be" in front of the verb. "To be" and its forms are weak verbs. All they indicate is existence. They have no motion or sound. When you put these verbs in front of the action verbs, the results are passive voice verbs:

Passive	Active
is completed	complete
was prepared	prepare
were entered	enter
will be sent	send
are calculated	calculate

Notice what happened to the action verbs. Not only do they have extra words in front of them, but they usually need extra letters at the end of them to be grammatically correct.

Summary   A good way to recognize the passive voice is by a form of the verb "to be" followed by the past tense of the verb.

Prefer Active Voice Verbs

Perhaps the examples listed so far in this chapter illustrate some of the reasons why you should prefer the active voice.

Active voice is simpler and shorter.

Active voice defines responsibilities.

Active voice is more interesting.

Active Voice Is Simpler and Shorter   As the examples show, active voice uses the basic sentence structure of our language. Therefore, it is simple and easy to understand. Since passive voice adds words and letters, it makes sentences longer. Chapter 9 explained the value of shorter sentences.

Look back at Example 10.1. The active sentence has 6 words; the passive has 8. If all sentences have two extra, unnecessary words, imagine all the extra, unnecessary words in the manual!

In the passive sentence, you have to read the whole thing before you find out who is responsible for the task. The defining of responsibility brings us to the next reason for preferring active voice verbs.

Active Voice Defines Responsibilities   Look at the passive voice example again. That first passive sentence could be a worse passive sentence, the second one shown in Example 10.3. This is still a grammatically correct sentence. Passive voice verbs don't need direct objects. But this sentence can lead to a lot of problems. Who completes the input form?

Sentences like that one may lead every reader to think that someone else is responsible. A manual must define responsibilities, and active voice verbs do that best. The responsible person is the subject of the sentence.

Active Voice Is More Interesting   Active sentences have a more stimulating tone. They are direct and to the point. After all, your goal is to get people to read the manual and understand it. If it's too dull, people won't even read it.

Example 10.3   Passive Voice

The input form is completed by the clerk.

The input form is completed.

However, sometimes only passive voice can provide a necessary tone or connotation. Sometimes the action is more important than the performer of the action.

Write Sentences with Active Voice Verbs

Now that you know what active voice is and why it is better than passive voice, use active voice when you write your sentences. Three suggestions help you do that:

Start with the actor.

Start with the verb.

Don't start with "there."

Start with the Actor   If the first word in your sentence is the person performing the action, you will be forced to use an active voice verb. Thus, the steps in writing each sentence would be:

1. Name the person responsible for the action.
2. Name the action.
3. Name the object acted upon.

Example 10.4   Starting Sentences with the Actor

Step 1	Step 2	Step 3
The clerk	completes	the input form.

Start with the Verb   If the manual is for only one audience, speak directly to that audience, as in Example 10.5.

Example 10.5   Starting Sentences with the Verb

Complete the input form.

Check the entries.

Send the form to the Data Entry Department.

Now we're down to only four words. The reader can't be confused about who is responsible. This kind of sentence is also conversational. If someone asked "What should I do first?," "Complete the input form" would be a natural, conversational response. This is the cookbook style explained in Chapter 6.

Look at the table of contents of this book. All of the chapter titles and headings are sentences that begin with verbs. If you read only the table of contents, you would have a list of procedures directed to you, this book's reader, the manual writer.

Even if the manual has more than one audience but you're using playscript style, use sentences that begin with the verb.

Example 10.6   Starting Sentences with the Verb, Playscript Style

CLERK	Complete the input form.
	Check the entries.
	Send the form to the Data Entry Department.
DATA ENTRY OPERATOR	Key the data.
	Verify the data.

Don't Start with "There"   "There" is an odd word. It's not a verb so it doesn't quite belong with a discussion of active versus passive voice verbs. But, like passive verbs, it requires a form of the verb "to be." It also adds little but clutter to a sentence and is dull. Therefore, this advice is part of this chapter.

Change Passive Voice Verbs to Active

Despite all your efforts, you will still write some passive sentences. Before you let a passive verb stay in your writing, try alternatives first. Try to rewrite the passive sentence with the subject or the verb first.

Summary   Always try to write sentences with active voice verbs.

Further References

Brogan, John A. *Clear Technical Writing.* New York: McGraw-Hill Book Company, 1973.
Chapter 4 has exercises for recognizing active and passive voice verbs and changing passive verbs to active.

Joseph, Albert. *Put It in Writing.* Cleveland, Ohio: The International Writing Institute, Inc., 1979.
This book offers many suggestions for clear writing and expands upon the ideas presented in this book. Mr. Joseph focuses on business writing and has written and conducted writing seminars for many companies.

The Manuals Corporation of America (MCA) (53 William Penn Drive, Stony Brook, New York, 11790) conducts seminars and provides material that can help with using the active voice.

Strunk, William Jr., and White, E. B. *Elements of Style.* New York: Macmillan Publishing Company, Inc., 1979.
See the section called "Use the active voice" in the chapter "Elementary Principles of Composition."

11

Use Effective Grammar and Punctuation

Rules of grammar and punctuation cannot be ignored. If you feel you need refreshers on the basics, use the references at the end of this chapter to brush up.

Grammar and punctuation have rules or standards because they help communication. When everyone uses the same rules, people understand one another better. Grammatical rules govern word forms and relationships. People who speak the same language agree to observe them so they can send and receive messages accurately. Thus, you must know and use these rules to achieve your goal.

This chapter offers some advice on using grammar and punctuation correctly. Perhaps the best advice for doing this was in Chapter 9, however. That chapter suggested using short words and sentences. When you keep your sentences short, correct grammar and punctuation are much easier.

Learn What Grammar Is

W. Somerset Maugham wrote,

> "It is well to remember that grammar is common speech formulated. Usage is the only test. I would prefer a phrase that was easy and unaffected to a phrase that was grammatical."

Grammatical rules are not written in stone, nor are they absolute natural laws. They are simply conventions based on language usage among English-speaking people. If enough people break one of those conventions enough times, then it is no longer a convention. Thus, it is no longer a grammatical mistake to break that convention. English teachers may persist in trying to uphold the old convention, but they are wasting their time.

Remember this when you are trying to follow grammatical rules. Some conventions still hold. Make sure your sentences are complete. They must have subjects and verbs, and the verbs must agree with the subjects. Plural subjects have plural verbs. Refer to plural nouns with plural pronouns. These are the basics.

Learning what grammar is means realizing what it isn't also. Some so-called "rules" were never real rules. A real grammatical rule promotes communication. For example, someone probably told you this "rule": "Never end a sentence with a preposition."

Prepositions are weak words, and the last word of a sentence is a strong place. Thus, a preposition at the end of a sentence is sometimes awkward or inappropriate. But that's not always true.

Winston Churchill was criticized once for ending a sentence in a preposition. His reply was,

> "This is the type of arrogant pedantry up with which I will not put."

Now, that's awkward! His point is well-taken. Sometimes it is much more awkward *not* to end a sentence in a preposition. Thus, this rule is not a rule at all; it doesn't promote communication.

The old rule probably grew out of the Latin root of the word "preposition." "Prepositio" means something that comes before. The reasoning must have been that if it comes before, it can't come at the end with nothing after it. But Latin rules don't necessarily apply to English.

Therefore, don't go out of your way to end a sentence in a preposition or to avoid doing so. Some sentences almost have to end in a preposition. However, most sentences need not end in prepositions.

Another "rule" said writers must never begin sentences with "and," "or," "but," "so," etc. These words are connectives. They take your reader from one thought to the next and explain the relationship between the two. Writing, and certainly speaking, is filled with sentences that begin with connectives.

Use Connectives

Beginning sentences with "and," "or," or "but" is not the only way to show the reader the connection between ideas. You can use other transitional words and phrases.

Connectives are like road signs that tell the reader which direction you are going. For example, some connectives are signs of a U turn: "however," "by contrast," "on the other hand."

Other connectives signal comparisons: "likewise," "similarly." Others signal logical arguments or conclusions: "since," "therefore," "thus." Others signal illustrations: "for example," "to illustrate." Others signal sequential relationships: "next," "later," "then." Others signal a conclusion or a restatement: "finally," "in conclusion," "to summarize."

Use the correct connective to convey your precise meaning. Don't give the reader the wrong direction. Connectives are useless if they are misused.

Use Commas Sparingly

Commas are important to understanding. They set apart introductory phrases, quotations, dates, parenthetical expressions, and words or phrases in a series. But commas can be used too often.

Use commas to set off parenthetical phrases and series. Don't use commas to separate ideas. Whenever you find yourself wondering if a sentence needs a comma to separate ideas, make two sentences. Remember that a sentence should have only one main idea. Compound and complex sentences need commas. But manuals need few, if any, compound or complex sentences. This relieves you from the chore of punctuating those long sentences.

The last comma in a series is optional. That is, you may write:

purchase orders, inventory, and income

or

purchase orders, inventory and income

Either is correct. Decide whether or not to use the last comma. Then use or don't use it consistently.

Speaking of series of words or phrases, make sure they all originate from the same word and that they all have the same grammatical structure. Examples 11.1 and 11.2 show series that are not correct because they do not have the same grammatical structure.

Example 11.1   Writing Series

> Faulty: The commands enter, change, calculate, and one of them simply stops the system's processing.
> Improved: The commands enter, change, and calculate your data. One of them simply stops the system's processing.

In Example 11.1, the first three words in the series are single words. The last part of the series is a sentence by itself.

Example 11.2   Writing Series

> Faulty: The commands are used in entering, changing, and to calculate data.
> Improved: The commands are used in entering, changing, and calculating data.

In Example 11.2, "to calculate" is an infinitive and different grammatically from the gerunds "entering" and "changing." It is not essential for you to be able to name infinitives and gerunds. Simply have a good idea of what words go together. A good English usage handbook will help you.

Use Semicolons Sparingly

Few people know when to use semicolons. And most of those that do are English teachers. Even grammar books seem unsure of their

Example 11.3   Using Semicolons

> A paragraph is a sequence of sentences; a program is a sequence of statements.
>
> Enter the 6-digit date; use the 2-digit month, the 2-digit day, and the last 2 digits of the year.

uses. Grammar handbooks use words like "often," "unless," and "usually" when listing the uses for semicolons. Therefore, try not to use them. It's difficult to use them correctly.

The only time you may be tempted to use a semicolon is when two sentences are so closely related that a period is just too much separation.

Use Quotation Marks and Underlining Cautiously

Readers' eyes are attracted to quotation marks and underlining. Thus, don't overdo either one. Manuals seldom need direct quotations or other standard uses of quotation marks.

You'll be tempted, when writing the input form instructions or report descriptions, to put all the headings in quotation marks. Think how cluttered with quotation marks the pages will be! It's better to write the headings exactly as they appear on the form or report and leave out the quotation marks.

It gets even worse if you enclose user-entered data in quotation marks. That may be a legitimate and grammatically correct use of quotation marks, but it still clutters the page. Find a neater way of indicating user-entered data. Chapter 8 suggested using capitals and underlining, italics, or boldface.

Like quotation marks, underlining clutters the page. If you use the convention suggested in Chapter 8 to underline or use boldface or italics for user-entered data, then use that convention for only those items. It ruins the convention to italicize or underline anything else. Thus, that convention eliminates underlining for emphasis. (Capital letters, like "NOTE:," are alternatives to underlining for emphasis.)

Even if you don't use the convention to underline or use boldface or italics for user-entered data, be careful about using those devices for emphasis too often. They will lose their impact. The effect will be the same as for the boy who cried, "Wolf!" The readers will begin to ignore what you are trying to emphasize.

Summary   Know and understand the basics of good grammar. Combine this with common sense and visual sense to know what sounds right and is pleasing to the eye.

Further References

Bernstein, Theodore M. *The Careful Writer, a Modern Guide to English Usage.* New York: Atheneum, 1966.
This book helps with word choice and enables the writer to select the word with the most precise meaning.

Burger, Robert S. "How to Write So People Can Better Understand You." *The Journal of Accountancy,* July, 1974.
This article explains what grammar is and how traditional English class rules may not be true rules of grammar.

Evans, Bergen, and Evans, Cornelia. *Dictionary of Contemporary American Usage.* New York: Random House, 1957.
This is an up-to-date handbook for grammar, punctuation, etc.

Joseph, Albert. *Put It in Writing.* Cleveland, Ohio: The International Writing Institute, Inc., 1979.
This book offers many suggestions for clear writing and expands upon the ideas presented in this chapter. Mr. Joseph focuses on business writing and has written and conducted writing seminars for many companies.

Strunk, William Jr., and White, E. B. *Elements of Style.* New York: Macmillan Publishing Company, Inc., 1979.
Use the chapter called "Elementary Rules of Usage."

Walsh, J. Martyn, and Walsh, Anna Kathleen. *Plain English Hand-*

book. Columbus, Ohio: McCormick Mathers Publishing Company, 1959.
This is a good, basic grammar and usage handbook.

Wooley, Edwin C., Scott, Franklin W., and Bracher, Frederick. *College Handbook of Composition.* Boston: D. C. Heath and Company, 1958.
This is a basic handbook for grammar and usage.

Write Each Section of the Documentation

Your table of contents defines each section of the manual or documentation. This section of the book offers guidelines for writing those sections. Your documentation may have more, fewer, or different sections than those described here. You may call them by different names. But no matter what you have decided to include in your documentation, the sections described in this book should apply.

Not all documentation will have the order described here for its sections; this order is most appropriate for batch systems. A different sequence may be more appropriate for online systems. However, all systems have input, processing, and output. Apply the principles in these sections to writing about those aspects of the system.

The sections described here are the introduction (Chapter 12), the input instructions (Chapter 13), the operating instructions (Chapter 14), the output descriptions (Chapter 15), and the appendices (Chapter 16). Once the manual is written, you can finalize the table of contents (Chapter 17).

12

Write the Introduction

Keep the introduction brief! Don't burden the reader with nonessential preliminaries. Explain the purpose of the documentation, the purpose and capabilities of the system, and any conventions used in the documentation.

Limit the Scope

The scope of a microcomputer documentation may be broad, since the user may be unfamiliar with the subject area and with computers. Therefore, the documentation for packaged software should explain the subject area and some basics about computers. Documentation for in-house microcomputer applications can follow the same guidelines for other in-house documentation.

The scope of a microcomputer package's documentation expands if the package will apply to more than one kind of computer. Some functions or keystrokes may be slightly different depending on the microcomputer used. One version of the documentation would apply to an IBM-PC, another to an Apple, etc.

For typical business applications, the documentation should not have to explain the basics of the user's subject area. (It may have to explain some basics of data processing, however.) A user manual (even one whose purpose is training) is not a textbook. For example, in our inventory/purchase order system manual, we would not explain what purchase orders are or how the orders received affect inventory. We have to assume that someone using such a system knows the basics of that subject matter. If the user doesn't, the explanation belongs in another book. Even a training manual should be limited to training for use of the system, not training in the user's subject matter. However, state in the introduction that the users must understand the basics. Then, if they don't, they can obtain that knowledge elsewhere.

Tell users what forms they'll need. This helps them prepare for using the system. Tell them what reports they'll receive.

Provide an Overview

Since the documentation must be divided into small sections, the introduction may be the only place the user can get an overview of the entire system. Explain the interrelationships between the different sections and how they interact. This is especially important when the system is large and has many different kinds of data. Users must know how all the different parts fit together.

In our purchase order/inventory system, the introduction should explain that purchase orders eventually affect inventory. Since different people may be responsible for different kinds of data, the users may never realize how what they are doing affects the system as a whole.

Often a diagram helps users visualize the entire system. Chapter 21 explains the use of diagrams.

Use a Case Study

It is a good idea to have a case study as a consistent example. Then the reader can follow the case from data input, through processing, to output. The introduction should explain the fictitious organization or department used in the case study. Chapter 1 of this book introduced the Acme Distributing Company and the Wonder-Calc spreadsheet, the case studies in this book. Chapter 20 explains the use of a case study a little more.

Explain the Conventions

Chapter 8 explained using conventions and their value. The introduction must introduce and explain the conventions.

Guide the Use of the Documentation

Sometimes user documentation needs brief explanations of how to use it. This is especially true for manuals that have more than one audience or for manuals that serve as both training and reference manuals.

Tell users where to start and how to find information quickly.

Define Responsibilities

Especially when a manual has more than one audience, define who must do what. If some users need read only the input form instructions, explain that. If some users must understand the reports and need not be concerned with input data, explain that.

Checklist for Writing the Documentation's Introduction

Include the following in the Introduction.

1. Purpose of the documentation
2. Purpose of the system
3. Capabilities of the system
4. Knowledge required to use the system
5. Overview of the system
6. Introduction of the case study
7. Explanation of the conventions
8. Guidelines to using the manual
9. Definition of responsibilities

13

Write the Input Instructions

If users don't collect and enter their data correctly, nothing else in the system will be right. The system can't produce good reports from bad data. The saying "garbage in, garbage out" means that input is vitally important. The kind of system and its data entry capabilities determine how you write the input instructions.

Online systems use terminals for data entry. Terminals can have screens or can be printers with keyboards. However, the fact that data entry occurs at a terminal does not mean that the system is online. Data can be collected at a terminal and then transmitted to the computer for batch processing.

All online systems have a direct connection to the computer and check data as they are entered (interactive). Not all online systems, however, are real-time. Real-time systems receive, process, and return data almost immediately.

Batch systems usually require input forms or source documents to provide the data to be entered into the computer. Often, someone else may enter them. Even some online systems need input forms, so that data can be gathered before the user goes to the terminal. Online systems that don't need input forms often have prompting messages that appear on the screen or the terminal printer. They ask for the data that would otherwise be asked for on an input form. Often, the messages on the terminal look just like an input form. Other times, the system does not provide prompting messages. The users create files based on information they have gathered. In these cases, the system usually has a form for gathering the data. Real-time systems require that you explain to the user what will happen after data entry, since processed data will be transmitted to the terminal.

Microcomputer systems normally do not use input forms. The users enter data directly to the program in a similar way to online systems. However, new technology and some microcomputers offer more variety of methods for entering data. While these may appeal to the user, some may require a bit of sophistication to use.

For example, a mouse (or any other user interface) does not usually replace the keyboard. The mouse just replaces some typing on the keyboard. Other input media, such as light pens, allow users to hand-draw letters and numbers and even graphic images and input them into the computer.

For most business applications, the keyboard is the normal means of entering data. It is time-consuming to take your hands from the keyboard to use a mouse or a light pen or to touch the screen. Therefore, your user instructions will usually center on using the keyboard to enter data. But you must be prepared to write about other ways to enter data.

If voice command products have big enough vocabularies and recognize many voices and continuous speech, this method of data entry will become more popular. This and other methods of "hands-free" data entry are especially helpful when the users' hands are occupied and using the keyboard is impossible.

Barcode scanners are another way data can enter an application system. They are useful in any kind of tracking system from super-markets to delivery services.

Imagers can also capture data by scanning a piece of paper and storing the image. Card readers are another way to enter data. The user makes pencil marks on a card and enters data directly into the computer. Like these other alternative data entry methods, this method bypasses the keyboard. Card readers are especially pop-ular in educational applications. The writer must explain, in step-by-step instructions, how to enter data regardless of the medium used.

Most of this chapter will discuss input instructions by using the example of an input form. The advice here can be adapted easily to online data entry by thinking of the principles and steps involved.

Use Your Knowledge of the Computer System

Chapter 1 explained how to gain an understanding of the system. The sections of the functional specifications discussed in that chapter that will help you write the input form instructions are:

Input description

Data dictionary

Error messages

Interpret the functional specifications into language the user will understand. Example 13.1 shows how you could do this for the input description.

Example 13.1   Input Description

Functional Specifications:	Supplier company A30 else truncate
Documentation:	The supplier company name can be up to 30 characters. If more than 30 characters are entered, the computer will drop all characters after the thirtieth.

Include Examples

The old saying that a picture is worth a thousand words applies to user manuals. Include examples of *completed* input forms. Users probably have blank input forms. They need to see how a completed one looks.

Example 13.2 shows the blank input form for entering purchase order information.

This particular blank input form itself explains a lot. From it, users know the maximum size of their entries. They know the kinds of data required for an add. Their job is to gather these data and get the information into the computer system.

If this were an online system, the data names (PURCHASE

Example 13.2   Blank Input Form

```
                          Acme Distributing Company

                      Purchase Order/Inventory System

                        Purchase Order Input Form
                                (PO123)

Add   Change   Delete                    Name _____
  (circle one)                           Date _____

PURCHASE ORDER NUMBER:  |_|_|_|_|_|_|_|_|

DATE:  |_|_|_|_|_|_|

SUPPLIER CO.:  |_|_|_|_|_|_|_|_|_|_|_|_|_|_|_|_|_|_|_|_|_|_|_|_|_|_|_|_|_|_|

ITEM NUMBER:  |_|_|_|

QUANTITY:  |_|_|_|_|_|

COST/ITEM:  |_|_|_|_|_|·|_|_|
```

ORDER NUMBER, etc.) would probably appear on the terminal.
The boxes, however, would not appear on a screen. (Not all input
forms have boxes either.) Therefore, the user wouldn't be able to
determine the lengths of the entries. The manual must explain that.

Sometimes online systems' messages include hints about the
lengths, though. The prompting messages may be like those in Example 13.3.

Example 13.3   Prompting Messages

```
PURCHASE ORDER NO. (8 DIGITS):

DATE (6 DIGITS):

SUPPLIER CO. (30 CHARACTERS):

ITEM NUMBER (3 DIGITS):

QUANTITY (5 DIGITS):

COST (999.99):
```

Online systems that use commands sometimes have a HELP command. Users can enter HELP in reply to any system prompt. The system then displays the correct way to respond to the prompt. This provides an online user manual of sorts. Thus, HELP messages should be written in the same language user manuals are. But look how much more a completed form (or online prompting messages) will explain.

Example 13.4   Completed Input Form

```
                        Acme Distributing Company

                      Purchase Order/Inventory System

                        Purchase Order Input Form
                                (PO123)

Add    Change   Delete                   Name _____
  (circle one)                           Date _____

PURCHASE ORDER NUMBER:  |_|_|_|_|2|3|4|5|

DATE:  |0|3|2|6|8|2|

SUPPLIER CO.:  |A|B|C|_|C|O|_|_|_|_|_|_|_|_|_|_|_|_|_|_|_|_|_|_|_|_|_|_|_|_|

ITEM NUMBER:  |1|2|3|

QUANTITY:  |_|_|_|1|0|

COST/ITEM:  |_|_|1|0|.|0|0|
```

Now the user can see that the purchase order number is all numbers and can be less than 8 numbers. However, if it's less than 8 numbers, the last digit must still be in the eighth box. The supplier company name can be less than 30 characters. The quantity can be less than 5 numbers, etc.

Online systems' manuals should show completed examples also. A printout or a mocked-up display can show the prompting messages and example responses.

Provide Step-by-Step Instructions

To go with the example, write step-by-step instructions that follow the sequence of the input form (or prompting messages). Use the words and capitalization exactly as they are on the input form.

Example 13.5   Written Instructions for Input Form

1. NAME   Sign your name.
2. DATE   Enter today's date.
3. ADD CHANGE DELETE   Circle the appropriate word.
   a. If you are adding a purchase order, circle ADD and complete everything on the form.
   b. If you must change a purchase order, circle CHANGE and enter the purchase order number. Then enter only the changing information on the rest of the form.
   c. If you are deleting a purchase order, circle DELETE and enter the purchase order number. Leave the rest of the form blank.
4. PURCHASE ORDER NUMBER   On an add, enter a new purchase order number. Use up to 8 digits. The last digit must be in the last box. Check the Purchase Orders by P.O. Number Listing to make sure the number does not already exist.
      On a change or delete, enter the number of the purchase order that is changing or being deleted. That number must be the number of a purchase order that already exists.
5. DATE   Enter the current date using 6 digits; the 2-digit month, the 2-digit day, and the last 2 digits of the year. For example, March 26, 1982 is 032682.
6. SUPPLIER CO.   Enter the name of the company. Use up to 30 alphabetic or numeric characters. The computer will drop any characters after 30.
7. ITEM NUMBER   Use the 3-digit code assigned to the item being ordered. Check the Items by Item Number Listing for the number.
8. QUANTITY   Enter the number of items being ordered. Use up to 5 digits with the last digit in the last space.
9. COST/ITEM   Enter the cost of each item. Use up to 4 digits, a decimal point, and 2 decimal places.

The written instructions add more information. Now the users know how to handle adds, changes, and deletes. They know where to look for the system information they'll need.

In some online systems, the terminal may look like an input form, as in Example 13.6.

Example 13.6   Input on Terminal Screen

PURCHASE ORDER NUMBER:	A C D I E
DATE:	
SUPPLIER CO.:	
ITEM NUMBER:	
QUANTITY:	
COST/ITEM:	

Note that the basic difference between this and the input form is the letters in the upper right. Explain this as in Example 13.7.

Example 13.7   Instructions for Input on Terminal—Acme's Purchase Order/Inventory System

A   ADD. Put the cursor over the A to add a purchase order.

C   CHANGE. Put the cursor over the C to change a purchase order. The system will not allow you to change a purchase order number. The keys will lock up if you try.

D   DELETE. Put the cursor over the D to delete a purchase order.

I   INQUIRY. Put the cursor over the I to view a purchase order. The system will not allow you to change anything.

E   EXIT. Put the cursor over the E to stop what you are doing.

The rest of the instructions remain the same as for an input form.

When users are using a microcomputer package, they may not always have prompting messages for each kind of data. In these cases, the manual must explain how to enter data. Example 13.8 illustrates this.

When users build their own data entry files, they will not be responding to prompting messages. Instead, they usually transfer data from an input form to a computer file via the terminal. This requires great accuracy from the user. The manual can still provide

Example 13.8   Instructions for Input on Terminal—Wonder-Calc

After you load the Wonder-Calc program your screen will look like this:

Columns/ 1 2 3 4 5 6
Rows
    1
    2
    3
    4
    5
    6

COMMAND:

1. To enter heading for rows and/or columns, move the cursor to the spot where you want the heading to appear.

2. Press *T* for text. Enter the heading. Use the Width command, if necessary, to make the columns wider.

3. To enter number values within the rows and columns, define the format of the numbers (dollar values, percentages, etc.) using the Format command.

4. Press *N* for number. Enter the numbers.

step-by-step instructions even though the instructions cannot be as specific.

Files can be created in many ways. Sometimes users can choose the method they want to use. Other times the system requires a certain format. Terminals with screens may check the fields during data entry and allow for error correction. Other times the fields are not checked until an edit program checks the file. Learn exactly how the users should build the files. Provide step-by-step procedures and examples. When users create their own files, they must name the files. Explain the system's naming procedures. Often, users are also responsible for storing or purging the files they create. Give the procedures for storing and purging and advice about the cost of storage and the time for purging files safely.

The user of an online system must also know how to operate the terminal. Therefore, before you explain how to enter data, provide instructions about how to turn the terminal on and establish communications with the computer. Explain that the cursor on a screen indicates where data will be entered. If users must have passwords, explain how to enter the password or ID code.

Explain any messages that appear on the screen that are not part of the application system. For example, in an online system, messages from the computer's operating system software may occasionally appear on the user's screen. Explain when to expect such messages, what they mean, and what to do about them.

Summary   The combination of a completed input form, terminal printout, or screen and written instructions tell the user exactly how to enter data.

Checklist for Writing Input Instructions

1. Make the instructions appropriate to the type of data entry.
   a. Batch
   b. Online
   c. Real-time
2. Use step-by-step instructions based on the order of the input form, prompting messages, or input file.
3. Provide examples.

Further References

Roman, Daniel R. "Building Up Your Personal Computers—Part II: Data Input Devices," *Computer Decisions,* March, 1984, pp. 110–128.
This article explains the many alternatives available for input to microcomputers. The article describes several specific products and examples.

Documentation writers should read periodicals to keep their knowledge of the data processing industry current.

14

Write the Operating Instructions

If users complete input forms, the data must be transferred from the forms to the computer. Systems with user terminals allow the user to do this; other systems require that the input forms be sent somewhere else.

The operating instructions have to do with what happens to the data items once they are in the computer. Often, the users have no control over this. In these cases, computer operations personnel set up and schedule the jobs. The data items go through programs for checking and calculating, etc. However, if your manual's purpose is to explain the system to users who are uninvolved in computer operations, operating instructions need not be part of the manual.

In batch systems, the users usually only request processing or printing. For such systems, explain how to make the request. If a request form must accompany the input form or be sent to order a report, provide procedures for completing the request form.

However, some online systems (often time-sharing systems) allow the users themselves to execute a series of commands or instructions that operate the system. Such systems are explained here. User manuals for other kinds of systems may not need a chapter or section on operating instructions. It can just be a processing section.

The operating instructions are especially vital to online and microcomputer systems. The interaction between the user and the system is what makes the system work. When the user enters something, the system responds as the user or programmer has instructed it. The entries must be more precise and exact than when users complete input forms. With an input form, the user usually has a second chance. With entries on the screen, the system offers second chances only if the program recognizes the data as unacceptable. The response is immediate. Therefore, the user must know the correct entries to obtain the desired responses.

As technology changes, you may write explanations of new and special functions, such as "windows." (Windows allow users to split the screen and look at two or more different parts of the file or transactions at the same time.) How to use new capabilities will be part of the operating instructions. You must learn and understand such capabilities before you write about them.

To write the chapter on operating instructions, use the following sections and items from the functional specifications and your research:

Operations description

System messages
    Prompts
    HELP messages

Explain the Commands

Commands (also called transaction codes) control what happens to entered data in some online, interactive systems. Operating the system comes after data entry.

Users must understand each of the commands. At the beginning of the operating instructions, list all the commands, explain what they do, and tell the user when to use them.

The preceding chapter had an example of entering data online for our purchase order/inventory system case study. If that system were operated by user-entered commands, the Operating Instructions chapter would begin as shown in Example 14.1.

Such an overview explains to users what the commands are and when to use them. Note that the explanations connect the command name to its meaning. ("The ENTER command enters," "the SEARCH command searches," etc.) This makes the command name meaningful to the users. It might confuse them to say, "The

Example 14.1   List of Commands

The Purchase Order/Inventory system uses commands that enter data and then calculate and manipulate the data to produce reports. Select the appropriate commands according to what you want to do. Commands are:

ENTER   builds a data file and enters purchase order or items received data. Use this command to add new data. The system will ask what kind of data you are adding.

CHANGE   changes specific items of data on the file. Use this command to correct errors. The system will ask what you want to change.

CALCULATE   calculates the system's reports.

PRINT   prints selected reports. Use this command after you have added all the data (ENTER command), corrected them (CHANGE command), and performed calculations (CALCULATE command). The system will ask what reports you want to print.

SEARCH   searches for a specific item of data. Use this command to find and look at a specific item of data on your file. The system will ask you what you want to search for.

STOP   stops the terminal session. Use this command when you are done.

Each command has its own section in this chapter where it is explained in greater detail. Each command you enter causes the system to ask you questions so you can execute the command.

CALCULATE command *computes....*" Why not call it the COMPUTE command then?

The explanation allows users to plan their terminal sessions. The longer the terminal sessions are, the more online systems cost to use. Thus, you will be doing the users a favor by helping them plan while they are not using valuable computer time.

Provide Step-by-Step Instructions

Even though the online system will prompt the user through each command, the manual should contain those prompting messages also. Write the message with all the acceptable responses beneath it. This permits planning.

Often a specific response to one prompt causes another prompt. Sometimes, this can be quite complicated. You may have to be creative to find a clear way to explain the various alternatives and relationships. Often a diagram can help. (See Chapter 21.)

Present the explanations of the commands in the sequence the user will follow. If more than one sequence is possible, present the most typical sequence first. Then explain deviations from that sequence.

In our case study, the order of explanation would probably be the order the commands are listed in Example 14.1. The user would first enter the data (ENTER command), then change them if necessary (CHANGE command), then perform calculations (CALCU-LATE command), and then ask for reports (PRINT command).

An example of the PRINT command instructions follows.

Example 14.2   Step-by-Step Operating Instructions

PRINT Command

The PRINT command prints selected reports. The system prompts

　　COMMAND?

Enter PRINT.

The system prompts

　　REPORTS?

ALL prints all purchase order, inventory, and income reports.

PO prints purchase order reports only.

INV prints inventory reports only.

INC prints income reports only.

Purchase Order Reports

If you enter PO, the system will ask which purchase order reports you want to print.

PO REPORTS?

ALL prints all purchase order reports.

ORD prints purchase orders that have not been received. It prints items on order only.

REC prints purchase orders for which the merchandise has been received.

If you enter ORD, the system asks which order reports you want.

PO ORD REPORTS?

ALL prints all four reports listed below.

NUM prints purchase orders in purchase order number sequence.

DAT prints purchase orders in date ordered sequence.

CO prints purchase orders in alphabetic order by supplier company.

ITM prints purchase orders in item number sequence.

If you entered REC to the prompt, PO REPORTS?, the system will ask which received reports you want.

PO REC REPORTS?

ALL prints the five reports listed below.

NUM prints purchase orders received by purchase order number.

IN prints purchase orders received by invoice number.

CK prints purchase orders received by the check number used to pay the invoice.

ITM prints purchase orders received by item number.

CO prints purchase orders received by supplier company.

Inventory Reports

If you entered INV to the prompt, REPORTS?, the system will ask which inventory reports you want to print.

INV REPORTS?

ALL prints all inventory reports.

ITM prints the inventory by item number.

REO prints the items in inventory that have fallen below their pre-determined minimum levels. These are items for reorder.

VAL prints a summary report of the total value of items in inventory.

Income Reports

If you entered INC in response to the prompt, REPORTS?, the system will ask which sales income reports you want to print.

INC REPORTS?

ALL prints all sales income reports.

ITM prints sales income by item number.

CST prints a comparison between cost of items and sales income.

For microcomputer packages, the step-by-step instructions would be similar.

The step-by-step instructions will help the user plan. When users are sitting at online terminals, they may not have time to plan. Then, more than ordinarily, time equals money, because when a user is online to a computer, computer time, as well as user time, is being spent. Although employee time is often more expensive than computer time, companies don't want to waste money. Even though computers help employees, planning on computer time wastes money.

On many time-sharing networks, if users are idle for too long, the network automatically signs users off the system. Thus, planning prior to a terminal session is even more important.

Usually, such an online system has a HELP command, and

the user can enter HELP in response to any prompt. The system will then print something similar to what is in Example 14.2. The advantage to having it in the manual is that the computer usage costs are less. Printing the HELP messages uses computer time. Storing lengthy HELP messages in the computer can also be expensive. It is impossible for users to make their own notes when they have online user documentation.

The advantage of the HELP message is that it gives an immediate response to a specific question. The manual must explain all the alternative paths to responses for each prompt. Users have to find the paths they want in the manual. At the terminal, HELP messages will guide them along those paths.

Summary   Online user documentation for online systems can be very helpful and very expensive. Provide the users with alternative sources of information. Put these in the manual and in the system.

Include Examples

At the end of each command explanation, include an example of a typical use of that command. Use your case study to produce the examples.

An example of our PRINT command follows.

Example 14.3   Use of PRINT Command

COMMAND? *PRINT*

REPORTS? *PO*

PO REPORTS? *ITM*

COMMAND? *STOP*

Note that the example goes back to the original command of the system. The example starts and ends with the COMMAND? prompt. This way, you don't leave the users hanging.

Checklist for Writing Operating Instructions

1. List and explain all commands first.
2. Give step-by-step procedures for each command.
3. Include every possible response.
4. Include every possible prompt and the conditions under which it will appear.
5. Include examples that begin and end with the basic prompt of the system.

15

Write the Output Descriptions

The end product of any system is the information it produces. Users must be able to read, use, and interpret output correctly.

Output can be charts, reports (hard copy), displays on terminal screens, graphs, computer-drawn pictures (computer graphics), etc. Explain every kind of output that the system can produce.

Since people who use microcomputer packages often design their own reports, a separate section for output may not be necessary. If the package has pre-defined output, the suggestions in this chapter will apply to the microcomputer package. The system or package you are writing about may involve a report writer. This kind of software allows users to print or display reports that they design. If that capability exists, the output section should explain how to use it.

Often the users of output are different from the users who enter the data. If that is the case, write the output description for those users. Use language for them. Some people receive the output but don't interpret it. Tell the users who receive it what to do with it. Tell them how to distribute the output. Tell them how or where to file the output.

To write the descriptions, use the following sections and items from the functional specifications and your research:

Output description

Report layouts

Calculations

Explain Each Part of the Output

This may not always be necessary. Well-designed output should be self-explanatory. Column headings and titles should be descriptive enough to explain themselves.

However, this is not always true. Space limitations on paper or screens often require that headings be abbreviated. In these cases, explain all the headings. Use the abbreviation from the report heading; then give the unabbreviated description.

For example, the report headings for a purchase order listing report in the purchase order/inventory system may be as shown in Example 15.1. These may seem self-explanatory to you because you've been working with the system. But don't assume the users will understand them. Users often complain that computers abbreviate everything. That's true; and the least we can do is explain those abbreviations. So include that explanation.

Example 15.1   Output Headings and Explanation

PO#   ITM#   QUAN   SUPP. CO.   CST   TOT

PO#   Purchase Order Number. The first column lists all the purchase order numbers in purchase order sequence.

ITM#   Item Number. The second column lists the item number that identifies the item ordered.

QUAN   Quantity. The third column lists the number of items ordered.

SUPP CO   The fourth column is the supplier company.

CST   Cost. The fifth column lists the cost of each item.

TOT   Total. The sixth column is the total cost for that purchase order.

Not all computer output will take such a simple format, however. Computers produce all kinds of output. For example, computer graphics equipment combines graphic communication and computers. The printed results are colorful graphs, maps, charts, etc. Users may prefer this kind of output because they feel that charts show relationships better. This helps users in the areas of spotting trends and making decisions.

Other output is not as visual. It may be music or lighting effects. Sometimes users may use light pens or plotters to manipulate the output. The nature of the output determines the explanation in the manual.

Some computer output needs no explanation. When the screen flashes "GAME OVER" at the end of a computer game, all users will know what that means.

Sometimes, however, the beginnings and endings of a printed report contain some computer information that is completely mysterious (and sometimes useless) to the user. The report's first few pages may have run numbers, JCL (job control language), run time, etc., that are necessary for computer department control. But what is necessary to computer department personnel may be only confusing to users. If it is impossible to remove this part of the computer printout before it gets to the user, tell the user what it is, as in Example 15.2.

Example 15.2   Job Control Language Explanation

> Several pages of computer information and blank pages will precede your report. Look for the report title and PAGE 1. If the report is corrrect, remove the beginning pages and discard them.
>
> If the report is not correct or has other problems (old data, for example), save those pages. Return them and the report to the Computer Department with an explanation of the problem. The extra pages will help Computer Department personnel trace the problem.

Similar kinds of extra information may follow the report. Again, warn the user that it will be there. Tell them EOJ means "end of job." Tell them to discard any blank pages.

Include Examples

Examples should have actual figures, not just 9's. Programmers usually use 9's to represent numeric data. Actual data will never be all 9's. Use the system and your case study to produce real reports with meaningful numbers.

The report layouts you use for the source of your information may look like Example 15.3.

Example 15.3   Report Layout

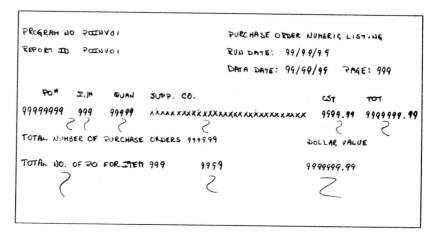

Those little x's and 9's don't mean much to the user. A detailed report, such as Example 15.4, does.

Example 15.4   Report

PROGRAM NO	POINV01	PURCHASE ORDER NUMERIC LISTING		
REPORT ID	POINV01	RUN DATE: 05/03/82		
		DATA DATE: 04/30/82 PAGE: 1		
PO#	ITM	QUAN	SUPP. CO.	CST TOT
00329814	2	10	ABC COMPANY	25.00 250.00
00329815	3	5	XYZ COMPANY	15.00 75.00
00329816	4	75	ABC COMPANY	10.00 750.00
TOTAL NUMBER OF PURCHASE ORDERS		90	DOLLAR VALUE	
			1075.00	
TOTAL NO. OF PO FOR ITEM 2		1	250.00	
TOTAL NO. OF PO FOR ITEM 3		1	75.00	
TOTAL NO. OF PO FOR ITEM 4		1	750.00	

Explain Any Balancing and Control Procedures

Often, when a system's purpose is financial or involves calculations, totals from output should be checked with manual totals. Explain where to find the computer's totals on output and how to balance them with the user's totals. Include possible reasons for out-of-balance conditions. Explain how to correct out-of-balance conditions and how to request a new report if necessary. (This would not apply to most microcomputer applications.)

Sometimes users should keep a log of the output received. Explain how to complete this control log.

Example 15.5   Control Log

Report Requested	Req. Date	Date Rec.	Computer Total	Manual Total	Differ.

The instructions for completing such a form could be as shown in Example 15.6.

Example 15.6   Control Log Completion Instructions

Report Requested	Enter the name or number of the report you requested.
Req. Date	Enter the date you requested the report.
Date Rec.	Enter the date you received the report.
Computer Total	Enter the total figure that appears on the report.
Manual Total	Enter the total you computed for the same figures.
Differ.	Enter any difference between the two totals. If a difference exists, determine the cause of the difference and correct the error.

Explain What to Do with Edit Reports or Error Listings

Thus far, we have been discussing output that is the final product of the system. But many systems that are not online produce edit reports or error listings. (Online systems often spot errors immediately and allow immediate correction or recognition.) Edit reports result from programs that check all the data that enter the system. If something is entered incorrectly, the edit report prints the data and an error message. The user must interpret the error message and correct the data. Online systems may also produce error messages on the terminal.

Regardless of the time lapse between data entry and editing, the feedback is essential. A user manual must explain each error message and what to do to correct the error.

However, the output section of the manual may not be the best place to do that. The output section should say that an edit report results when data are entered. But error correction must take place before the final output is produced.

Therefore, explain error correction where it will be most helpful to the user. Where that is depends on the system. If you've divided the manual by data types, error correction belongs with each data type. Other times, error correction may be more appropriately placed in an appendix. Chapter 16 explains how to write error messages in an appendix. The same writing technique would apply no matter where you include error correction.

Checklist for Writing Output Description

1. Tell users what to do with output.
2. Explain abbreviated headings.
3. Explain what to do with extra pages of printout.
4. Use actual reports, not report layouts.
5. Don't explain error messages and corrections in this section of the manual.

16

Write the Appendices

Appendices should include any information that is not essential to the step-by-step procedures but that the user may want to know.

Calculation detail may be important to the user. Yet, use of the system does not require knowing or understanding the formulas included in the system's programs. Therefore, if you feel that calculations should be part of the manual, include them in an appendix.

To use time-sharing systems, users must know how to access the time-sharing network. This is not really part of the actual system. But the user needs to know this information. Put it in an appendix. If you write several manuals for the same time-sharing network, this appendix can be the same in all your manuals.

If an online system creates files, list those files in an appendix. Users should know what files are stored so they can delete any they don't need.

Other uses for appendices are explained in more detail in the following subsections.

Explain Error Messages and Error Corrections

As stated earlier, this information need not be in an appendix. Often, however, an appendix is the most appropriate place to put it. When the manual is organized by type of data, error messages can be in the appropriate section. Even then, however, they may clutter the text with information that is the exception rather than typical.

Although error correction procedures are vital to use of the system, errors mean that the user did not follow the input instructions correctly. In that sense, error messages and error correction are outside of the normal step-by-step procedures.

Always explain error correction in terms of the error messages, because error messages alert users that an error exists. Therefore, they must be able to look up the message and find out what to do to correct the error.

List all possible error messages in some logical order. Often this order is alphabetic. Some systems assign numbers to all messages. Then, numeric sequence is more appropriate.

List the message, the reason it occurred, and what to do to correct the error, as shown in Example 16.1. Although this example applies to the purchase order/inventory system, the same format and principles can be used for microcomputer packages.

Example 16.1   Error Message Explanation

Error Message	Explanation	Correction
PO ALREADY ON FILE	You tried to add a purchase order number that is already on file.	Check the number you entered with what was keyed. If it was keyed incorrectly, re-submit the input form.
		Check the Purchase Order by Purchase Order Number listing to find a number that is not on file. Assign a new number. Re-submit the entry.
PO NOT NUMERIC	The purchase order number entered contains letters or other non-numeric characters. The purchase order number must be 8 digits.	This may have been keyed wrong. If so, re-submit the input form. If the number is wrong on the input form, correct it and re-submit.

Differentiate between error messages and warning messages. Many systems print error messages when the data cannot enter the system. They print warning messages when some non-essential data are missing or incorrect. Users must understand that a warning message does not prevent the data from entering the system. If the computer enters its own data in such cases (a default value), users must understand what is happening. Users may want to change what the computer entered.

Example 16.2   Warning Message Explanation

Warning Message	Explanation	Action
PO OUT OF SEQUENCE	The purchase order number is not one number higher than the previous one.	Make sure that no purchase orders are missing.
DATE MISSING DEFAULT = 000000	The computer will accept an entry without a date. It enters zeros in the date column.	Although the purchase order is in the computer, change the record by adding the correct date as soon as possible.

To write this section or appendix, use the error messages and input instructions. The explanation of the error message can repeat the input instructions for that data item.

Never simply list error messages. Users already know what they are or they wouldn't be looking them up.

Write a Glossary

Some data processing terms or even some terms that apply to the system's subject should be explained. Even though you explain some terms in the text, the user may not remember. When the manual is primarily for reference, you cannot assume that the user read the part where you defined the terms.

Therefore, a glossary will help users understand the manual.

If you must use terms like the following in the manual, include them in a glossary.

Code

Data

Data base

File

Hardware

Online

Offline

Program

Record

Software

System

Time-sharing

Put the glossary in alphabetic order. It is not really a dictionary. You need not include pronunciation. Provide only one definition, not several as a dictionary might. Provide only the definition that applies to the way you use the word. For a microcomputer package, list any words unique to that package as well as basic computer terminology. Be as basic as possible, since the users may be completely new to computers. Explain "cursor," "field," "message," "scroll," "diskette," "floppy disk," "mouse," "cassette," etc.

List the Command and/or Functions

For a large business system, it may be best to list the commands and functions in the operating instructions section of the user documentation. However, a microcomputer package manual may not have a separate operating section. The users will reference the commands and functions as they need them. Therefore, you may want to list them in alphabetic order in an appendix or separate reference section.

Provide Guidance

Often, any documentation, especially manuals for microcomputer packages, should include helpful hints. An appendix may be the best place for such guidance.

For example, microcomputer users need to know how to care for their diskettes or cassettes. They want to know how to use them efficiently and get as much information on them as possible. Tell the users how to keep the spreadsheet, for example, as compact as possible to use the storage medium efficiently and to lessen calculation time.

Remind users about the importance of backing up their data by creating copies. Include any advice that will help users become more efficient and keep their data secure. (See the Glossary at the end of this book.)

Compile an Index

An index is a helpful addition to a reference manual. Ask yourself what questions the users might ask. Think of what words they would use to ask them.

Then find every occurrence of the words or phrases and list the pages where they occur. Include cross-references to topics associated with the word and specific details that explain the reference.

A word processor can be a big help in compiling an index. See Chapter 21.

Summary   Write an appendix for any information not essential to the text but helpful to the user.

17

Finalize the Table of Contents

When the manual is completely written and typed with page numbers, finalize the Table of Contents. Until now, you've used your working Table of Contents as an outline. Only after the manual is done can you have a real Table of Contents.

Include All Headings and Sub-Headings That Appear in the Text

Every heading should be part of the Table of Contents. This makes the Table of Contents an easy-to-refer-to outline of the entire man-

Example 17.1   Chapter Table of Contents

Chapter 3   Input Instructions
            Operating the Terminal
                On/Off Switch
                Keyboard
            Commands

                ENTER Command
                CHANGE Command
                CALCULATE Command
                PRINT Command
                SEARCH Command
                STOP Command

ual. (See the Table of Contents for this book.) If the manual has too many headings and you feel the Table of Contents is too long, move the lower level headings to the beginning of each chapter as a chapter Table of Contents.

Indent Each Level

The chapter title can be flush with the left margin. Indent each subsequent level three spaces. Although five spaces is a normal indentation, a three-space indentation allows more room. If you have long headings, by the time you get to the third level of heading, it may not fit on one line. If you include more than three levels of headings, it is even more important to have the shorter indentation.

Make the Table of Contents Match the Headings

The wording and capitalization in the Table of Contents should match exactly what is in the manual.

Use Small Roman Numerals as Page Numbers

The rest of the manual must have page numbers before you can finalize the Table of Contents. Since the Table of Contents isn't done yet, you don't know how many pages it will be.

Therefore, start numbering the first page of the manual with 1. Number the pages of the Table of Contents with lower case Roman numerals: i, ii, iii, iv, v, etc.

Include a List of Examples and Illustrations

Sometimes, users may want to refer to a sample input form or report. It helps to have a list of the examples and illustrations included in the manual. Start this list on a separate page. Continue the numbering scheme from the Table of Contents. If the Table of Contents ends on page v, the example list would begin on page vi.

Summary   Remember that the final Table of Contents must be the last thing written. Before it can be finalized, the text of the manual must be finalized. Therefore, don't write the Table of Contents until all the graphics are completed and the manual is reviewed and all the corrections are made.

Use Examples, Diagrams, and Illustrations

Section 4 of this book stressed the importance of examples to illustrate what the user must do. Section 5 goes into greater detail about those examples and illustrations.

A case study should be the source of examples and illustrations. From the case study, prepare examples (Chapter 18) and diagrams and illustrations (Chapter 19).

18

Use Examples

As we've already seen, examples are often the clearest and most concise way to present and interpret information. Their quality and placement can increase their effectiveness.

Use a Case Study

We mentioned that a case study can enhance users' understanding of a system. A case study shows the users how data will look when entered and when processed. It is the best possible example of the system.

Develop a Typical Case User representatives and data processing personnel should get together and develop a fictitious organization or department that represents a typical application. Having both users and data processors participate in the development of the case study ensures that it is technically correct in both aspects. Users know the subject, and the programmers know the system. The data should be realistic. Although the case should be typical and realistic, include as many different kinds of situations as possible. This makes the case study more useful. If necessary, include more than one case study.

In developing the case study, follow these steps:

1. Make up the data.

2. Complete input forms, if applicable. Copy them.

137

3. Enter the data.

4. Use the computer system to process the data.

5. Copy the output. (For output that appears on a screen, type what appears on the screen or photograph the screen.)

Provide Sufficient Data   The case study should include enough data to produce meaningful output. Too much data will make the output too long to serve as useful examples. The actual system and its application will determine how much data to use in the case study. You, the user, and the programmer or project leader must use your judgment to define sufficient data.

Show the Case Study from Beginning to End   The case study should run throughout the manual: from data input, to processing, to output.

The completed input forms should be the examples with the input description. If data entry is online via a terminal with a screen, typed copies or photographs of the screens should also be part of that section.

For interactive, online systems in which the user operates the system, copies of that interaction should be the examples in the operating instructions section of the manual.

Copies of the output should be the examples in the output description section of the manual.

Thus, the entire case study is used in the appropriate place. An appendix could include all the examples without text. This allows users to see the system in action. They can see what happens to data that enter the system.

While a case study is an asset to any manual, it is especially important in a training manual.

Checklist for Using a Case Study

1. Develop the case study with users and programmers.

2. Make sure it is technically correct.

3. Include sufficient, realistic data.

4. Include input, processing, and output with the same data.

Place Examples Near the Written Explanation

The placement of examples of input forms is especially important. The example should be as close as possible to the instructions that explain how to complete the form. Otherwise users have to flip back and forth between pages to see how the instructions relate to the actual form.

Sometimes the example input forms can be reduced and placed within the text, as in Example 18.1.

Example 18.1   Putting Example within Instructions

1. NAME   Sign your name.
2. DATE   Enter today's date.
3. ADD CHANGE DELETE   Circle the appropriate word.
   a. If you are adding a purchase order, circle ADD and complete everything on the form.
   b. If you must change a purchase order, circle CHANGE and enter the purchase order number. Then enter only the changing information on the rest of the form.
   c. If you are deleting a purchase order, circle DELETE and enter the purchase order number. Leave the rest of the form blank.

```
                    Acme Distributing Company

                  Purchase Order/Inventory System

                    Purchase Order Input Form
                            (PO123)

Add    Change    Delete            Name _____
   (circle one)                    Date _____

PURCHASE ORDER NUMBER:  |_|_|_||2|3|4|5|

DATE:  |0|3|2|6|8|2|

SUPPLIER CO.:  |A|B|C|_|C|O|_|_|_|_|_|_|_|_|_|_|_|_|_|_|_|_|_|_|_|_|_|_|_|_|_|_|_|

ITEM NUMBER:  |1|2|3|

QUANTITY:  |_|_|_|1|0|

COST/ITEM:  |_|_|1|0|.|0|0|
```

4. PURCHASE ORDER NUMBER   On an add, enter a new purchase order number. Use up to 8 digits. The last digit must be in the last box. Check the Purchase Orders by P.O. Number Listing to make sure the number does not already exist.

On a change or delete, enter the number of the purchase order that is changing or being deleted. That number must be the number of a purchase order that already exists.

5. DATE   Enter the current data using 6 digits; the 2-digit month, the 2-digit day, and the last 2 digits of the year. For example, March 26, 1982 is 032682.

6. SUPPLIER CO.   Enter the name of the company. Use up to 30 alphabetic or numeric characters. The computer will drop any characters after 30.

7. ITEM NUMBER   Use the 3-digit code assigned to the item being ordered. Check the Item by Item Listing for the number.

8. QUANTITY   Enter the number of items being ordered. Use up to 5 digits with the last digit in the last space.

9. COST/ITEM   Enter the cost of each item. Use up to 4 digits, a decimal point, and 2 decimal places.

Often, however, the input form must be placed on a page by itself. In such cases, two-sided pages are best. Then, the example form can be on the left-hand page and the instructions can be on the right-hand page opposite the example. (See Example 18.2.)

However, this creates problems when the page before the example form is a left-hand page. No right-hand page exists, and you are forced to have a blank right-hand page. Blank right-hand pages are technically incorrect to publishers and printers and usually look like mistakes. Try to arrange your text so you can get around this problem. When it is unavoidable, some manuals print, "This page intentionally left blank," or "Sample Purchase Order Input Follows," on what would otherwise be a blank right-hand page.

Make Examples Stand Out

Enclose examples in a box or shade the example. This will make the examples stand out in the text.

Example 18.2 Putting Example Beside Instructions

1. **NAME** Sign your name.
2. **DATE** Enter today's date.
3. **ADD CHANGE DELETE** Circle the appropriate word.
   a. If you are adding a purchase order, circle ADD and complete everything on the form.
   b. If you must change a purchase order, circle CHANGE and enter the purchase order number. Then enter only the changing information on the rest of the form.
   c. If you are deleting a purchase order, circle DELETE and enter the purchase order number. Leave the rest of the form blank.
4. **PURCHASE ORDER NUMBER** On an add, enter a new purchase order number. Use up to 8 digits. The last digit must be in the last box. Check the Purchase Orders by P.O. Number Listing to make sure the number does not already exist.

   On a change or delete, enter the number of the purchase order that is changing or being deleted. That number must be the number of a purchase order that already exists.
5. **DATE** Enter the current data using 6 digits; the 2-digit month, the 2-digit day, and the last 2 digits of the year. For example, March 26, 1982 is 032682.
6. **SUPPLIER CO.** Enter the name of the company. Use up to 30 alphabetic or numeric characters. The computer will drop any characters after 30.
7. **ITEM NUMBER** Use the 3-digit code assigned to the item being ordered. Check the Item by Item Listing for the number.
8. **QUANTITY** Enter the number of items being ordered. Use up to 5 digits with the last digit in the last space.
9. **COST/ITEM** Enter the cost of each item. Use up to 4 digits, a decimal point, and 2 decimal places.

Acme Distributing Company
Purchase Order/Inventory System
Purchase Order Input Form
(PO123)

Name _____
Date _____

Add   Change   Delete
(circle one)

PURCHASE ORDER NUMBER: |_|_|_|1|2|3|4|5|

DATE: |0|3|2|6|8|2|

SUPPLIER CO.: |A|B|C| |C|O| |_|_|_|_|_|_|_|_|_|_|_|_|_|_|_|_|_|_|_|_|_|_|_|_|

ITEM NUMBER: |1|2|3|

QUANTITY: |_|_|_|1|0|

COST/ITEM: |_|1|0|.|0|0|

Shaded examples are very attractive. They look professional and highlight the examples well. However, they are more difficult and expensive than boxes. If you do the shading yourself, press type is available that can be rubbed onto the paper. This may be tricky. Printers can also provide shading. Ask for a 10–15% screen.

Boxes are easier. Simply draw a box around the example. If you have a good eye and a good straightedge, you may be able to do this yourself with satisfactory results.

However, getting the lines straight and the corners even is more difficult than it seems. It is often worth having a graphic artist draw the boxes around the examples.

Make sure you leave enough margin room in the typed text for examples with shading or boxes.

Produce Good-Quality Originals

The examples will be reproduced in copies of the manual. Therefore, the original example must be of excellent quality.

For input forms, use a fine, black, felt-tipped pen to complete the example. Don't use blue ink; it doesn't copy well.

For examples of online system processing on a terminal with a screen, type the example so it looks as much as possible the way it would look on the screen. Use an OCR (Optical Character Recognition) typing font and a new ribbon. Type it on bond paper.

If the terminal has a printer, print an actual example. Use an impact printer, if possible. Put a new ribbon in the printer, and use plain, white paper. Don't use green bar computer paper; it doesn't reproduce well. Computer paper with lines makes the example look cluttered. Use plain, white paper for examples of reports also.

Indicate Breaks Clearly

If the example is too long to fit on one page, indicate in some way that the example continues. You could omit the line at the bottom of the box, as in this book. Or you could put wavy lines in the box or shading at the break. It is important that the user recognize where the beginning and end of the example are.

Reports can be hundreds of pages. Obviously, you would not want the entire report in the manual in such a case. But, if the end of the report has totals, it should be part of the example. Usually, one page of text is enough of an example for a report. Put wavy lines to indicate the break between the beginning and the end.

Example 18.3   Indicating Missing Material in Examples

PO#	ITM	QUAN	SUPP. CO.	CST	TOT
00329814	2	10	ABC Company	25.00	250.00
00329815	3	5	XYZ Company	15.00	75.00
00329816	4	75	ABC Company	10.00	750.00

Total Number of Purchase Orders	90		Dollar Value	
				1075.00
Total No. of PO for Item 2		1		250.00
Total No. of PO for Item 3		1		75.00
Total No. of PO for Item 4		1		750.00
Total No. of PO for Item 6		2		500.00
Total No. of PO for Item 9		3		300.00
Total No. of PO for Item 20		1		200.00

Provide Good Reductions

Often, you must reduce examples so they'll fit in the manual. Computer paper is wider than manual pages. Standard 8½- by 11-inch typing paper is only 80–96 characters wide. Therefore, computer examples must be reduced to fit on standard-size paper. Make sure that the reduction quality is good and that the example is still readable. Anything reduced below 64% is practically illegible; 77% is usually quite acceptable. Printers can provide better reduction quality than your office's copy machine.

Example 18.4   Reduced Computer Printout

```
PROGRAM NO  POINVO1                    PURCHASE ORDER NUMERIC LISTING

REPORT ID   POINVO1                    RUN DATE:  05/03/82

                                       DATA DATE: 04/30/82   PAGE:    1


    PO#    ITM    QUAN   SUPP. CO.                      CST      TOT
  00329814   2     10    ABC COMPANY                   25.00    250.00
  00329815   3      5    XYZ COMPANY                   15.00     75.00
  00329816   4     75    ABC COMPANY                   10.00    750.00

  TOTAL NUMBER OF PURCHASE ORDERS       90             DOLLAR VALUE
                                                          1075.00
  TOTAL NO. OF PO FOR ITEM   2          1                 250.00
  TOTAL NO. OF PO FOR ITEM   3          1                  75.00
  TOTAL NO. OF PO FOR ITEM   4          1                 750.00
```

Checklist for Using Examples

1. Put examples in the text or on the page opposite the explanation.

2. Box or screen examples.

3. Indicate breaks if examples won't fit on one page or are too long to be used in their entirety.

4. Use good-quality originals.

5. Use plain, white paper; not green-bar or lined computer paper.

6. Make sure any reduced examples are legible.

19

Use Diagrams and Illustrations

Charts and tables can help users understand the system. Most users can understand a diagram or an illustration of a process.

Use Procedures Flowcharts

These should not be data processing flowcharts. A procedures flowchart illustrates the steps a user would follow to perform a task.

In Chapter 14, Write the Operating Instructions, the PRINT command example (Example 14.2) had several branches or alternatives depending on the user's response. Perhaps a diagram would help users follow the path that their responses will take them along. See Example 19.1.

In developing such a diagram, use standard data processing flowcharting symbols as much as possible. However, don't use symbols that users may not understand. Users can understand if you use the rectangle to mean a process, a triangle to mean a decision, etc.

Use Tables

Another device for illustrating part of a system is a decision table or decision logic table. It expresses, in a compact form, the logical requirements of an aspect of the system. It shows what actions are possible under various conditions. Since some decision tables are very sophisticated, some users may have difficulty reading them.

Example 19.1   Procedures Flowchart

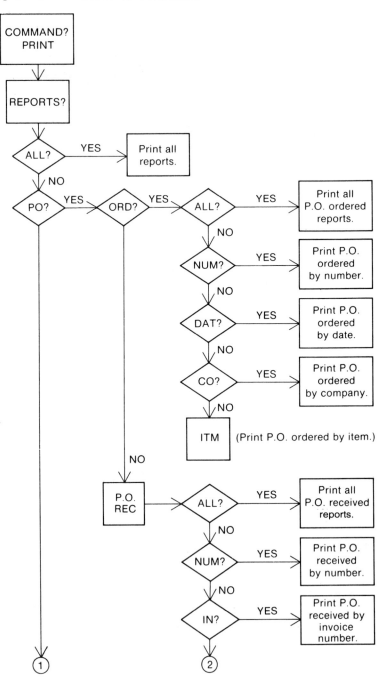

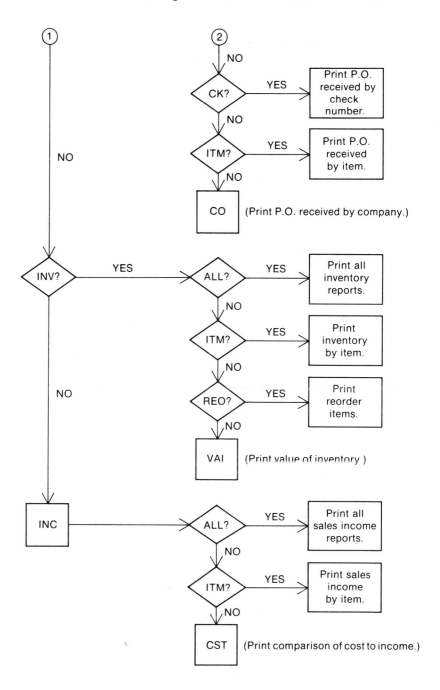

Make sure the users will understand the tables before using them.

If the decision table is simple enough, users should be able to understand it. Tax tables and different kinds of schedules will be familiar to users and are examples of decision tables. The tables represent "if" (condition) and "then" (action) statements. (If you earn $XXXXXX, then your tax is $XXX.) Such simple decision tables involve no more than two variables and are sometimes called result tables.

Example 19.2 is a simple version of a decision table. This table presentation may be easier for users to understand than the operating instructions example in Chapter 14 (Example 14.2) or the procedures flowchart in this chapter (Example 19.1).

Example 19.2   Decision Table

TO PRINT	ENTER
all reports	ALL
purchase orders	PO and
all purchase orders	ALL
purchase orders by number	NUM
purchase orders by date	DAT
purchase orders by company	CO
purchase orders by item	ITM
purchase orders received	REC and
all purchase orders received	ALL
purchase orders received by number	NUM
purchase orders received by invoice no.	IN
purchase orders received by check no.	CK
purchase orders received by item	ITM
purchase orders received by company	CO
inventory reports	INV and
all inventory reports	ALL
inventory by item	ITM
inventory for reorder	REO
value of inventory	VAL
income reports	INC and
all income reports	ALL
income by item	ITM
cost compared with income	CST

Summary   If the decisions the user must make are simple and have no more than two variables, use decision tables to illustrate the procedure.

Use Illustrations

Drawings and "cartoons" are effective ways to get your point across to the reader. Drawings may be especially helpful for some microcomputer applications. Cartoons are effective, especially when the subject matter is light or directed toward children.

A manual for a system that uses computer graphics should use illustrations because the system interaction between user and computer graphics is non-verbal. Sequences of illustrations, in color if possible, best convey the use of computer graphics.

Caption Each Diagram

Give a name to each example or illustration you use. Include that name in the list of examples and illustrations that follows the Table of Contents.

Place Diagrams Where They Are Most Useful

Put the diagram as close as possible to where you refer to it. If the user has to flip back and forth between pages, the chart will not be as useful. The PRINT command chart, for example, should accompany the PRINT command instructions.

Use Available Resources for Creating Diagrams

Perhaps you must create your own diagrams. If so, you'll need rulers and templates. However, you may have an artist available or the money to send the work to an artist.

If you are lucky enough to have computer graphics equipment available to you, use that resource. Computer graphics can prepare and present pictorial material on an interactive terminal. The principle uses of computer graphics are in the engineering design, architectural, marketing, planning, and scheduling areas, but the equipment can make colorful charts and graphs for your manuals.

Computer graphics capabilities are simply the creation and manipulation of pictures with the aid of a computer. Computer-controlled plotters produce the output on paper or film. Since general-purpose graphics packages are available, computer graphics may be valuable to manual writers. You may be able to use computer graphics for creating illustrations, diagrams, charts, etc.

Photographs are another good illustration device. Actual photographs of input or output will seem more real to the users. Photographs may be more expensive but more effective than drawn diagrams.

In conclusion, be as creative and imaginative as you can be to produce the most effective illustrations for your manual.

Type the Manual

At this point, you have a rough draft of the manual. That draft must be transformed into one that is suitable for review.

First, you must prepare the manual for typing (Chapter 20). The best way to type a manual is to use a word processor (Chapter 21). The best way to create an online "manual" is through the use of a documentation processor (Chapter 21).

20

Prepare the Manual
for Typing

The text is now complete but is handwritten or typewritten in rough form. That rough draft is marked up, words are crossed out, etc. In general, the rough draft is quite messy and hard to read.

Before you or someone else can type the documentation in a form suitable for review, you must prepare it for typing. This means cleaning it up and marking revisions so they are easy to understand. If you do your own typing, this may not be as important, provided you can read your own writing. However, if someone else is typing the documentation for you, a little more preparation is necessary.

Prepare the Draft for the Typist

If you have your own typist, meet with him or her and decide the best way to indicate changes. Work out a system that is easy for you to use and for the typist to interpret. Of course, it's best to have this meeting before you begin your rough draft. Then, you will make changes the agreed-upon way.

A rough draft of the system overview of the purchase order/ inventory system case study is shown as Example 20.1.

If you submit your rough draft to a steno or typing pool, find out what the pool's requirements are. Usually, a pool will accept only certain forms of drafts. Once you know how to prepare and mark a draft for typing, prepare the draft.

Example 20.1   Rough Draft, Typed with Corrections Indicated

System Overview

Acme Distributing Company's   *will*
The ˄ new purchase order/inventory system˄ keeps track of purchase orders.

When merchandise is received, the system will maintain the number and

value of items in inventory.

¶ *Order clerks will complete the purchase order input form that lists:*
˄Purchase order numbers / dates / supplier companies / Items / quantities,
and / costs ~~are entered on the input form.~~

¶ *Receiving clerks complete*   *lists:*
˄Another input form ~~is completed~~ when merchandise is received. It ~~has~~ ˄

/ purchase order numbers / dates / supplier companies / Items / quantities,

/ costs / Invoice numbers / and / check numbers

Dictate the Manual

If your company has some form of dictation capability, you may want to dictate the manual. You can dictate from your longhand draft or from a detailed outline.

Dictation requires skill. The skills needed depend on whether you dictate to a stenographer or to a machine. Whichever you use, learn how to dictate.

If a stenographer takes your dictation, meet with that person to find out the best way to dictate your material.

If you use machine dictation, know the capabilities of the machine. You must know how to correct mistakes and how to indicate format and layout requirements.

If you use any kind of dictation, remember to:

1. Speak slowly.
2. Spell proper nouns and any hard-to-spell words.
3. Differentiate between words that sound alike or could be misunderstood. For example,

   affect/effect

   counsel/council
4. Indicate punctuation, paragraphing, and indentation.
5. Indicate beginnings and ends of quotation marks, parentheses, and underlining.
6. Indicate special capitalization.

In summary, first drafts can be longhand, typed, or dictated. From its first draft, prepare the manual for typing in the way that best suits you, your typist, and the resources available to you. Sometimes machine dictation is not the best alternative, even if it is available to you. Consider the following when deciding the best way to prepare the manual for typing.

1. Prepare a longhand draft when:
   - a typist is available to you
   - special formats are part of the manual (They are easier to sketch than to explain verbally.)
   - the manual is long
2. Type it first when:
   - you are a good typist
   - a steno pool will accept only typed drafts
3. Dictate the manual to a stenographer when:
   - the typing requires much explanation
   - the stenographer is familiar with you and the type of work you are doing
4. Dictate to a machine when:
   - the manual is short
   - the manual has no complicated formats

21

Use the Automated Tools Available

Word processors, text processors, and documentation processors have replaced the typewriter as the best way to produce user documentation. Word and text processing include word processors and text-processing capabilities available on computers. A word processor is any typewriter that remembers what was typed on it and can retrieve that information. It captures text and stores it temporarily or permanently. It has the capability to retrieve the stored information so it can be changed. Setting margins, tabbing, backspacing, indenting, erasing, and all other ordinary typing tasks are done more quickly and efficiently. Other, not-so-ordinary typing tasks, like moving and copying text, are equally easy.

Text processing programs available on computers offer similar capabilities. Even microcomputers available for home and small business use have text processing capabilities. Since these microcomputers are quite inexpensive, every manual writer should use one. It would pay for itself before three manuals are completed.

Text processing is sometimes used synonymously with word processing. Usually, however, text processing (or text editing) implies the addition of features not normally part of word processing. Besides the normal word processing capabilities, text processing may include search and replace commands, graphics, pagination, mathematics, sort capability, automatic header and footer information, spelling verification, and communications.

The distinction between word, text, and data processing is fading. Many word processors can become text processors through an upgrade in software. Data processing functions, like mathematics and sorting, are part of text processing. The boundaries between copiers, word processing, typesetting, and reprographics are also less distinct.

These are no longer separate functions. Thus, this chapter uses the term "word processing" to mean any text-producing computer system.

Because a manual will rarely remain in its original form, word processing will save a great deal of time and effort.

Documentation processors differ from word processors, because they don't result in a hard-copy manual. Instead, they make user documentation available online.

A documentation processor is software that combines data base concepts with text processing concepts. It has advantages to both writers and users, as explained later in this chapter.

Understand the Capabilities

Whether you yourself or a word processing operator uses the word processor, know the capabilities.

Many word processors have what is called a glossary. A glossary stores frequently used words, phrases, or paragraphs. The operator can set up the glossary once, then, with only two keystrokes, "type" what is in the glossary. Whether you or an operator enters the text, you should know if the equipment has this feature. You can set up a glossary or help the operator set one up.

For example, in the case study, the phrase "purchase order/ inventory system" occurs often. Using the word processor's glossary, the operator would type the phrase once and assign it a code. Then, every time the phrase occurs in the text, the operator would press a glossary key (or its equivalent) and the code for the phrase. The phrase would appear in the text. This saves keystrokes and, consequently, time.

The search and replace capabilities can be especially helpful in a manual. If you decide to change every occurrence of a word to another word, the word processor can do it automatically. For example, you may realize that you called the computer system a "program" sometimes and a "system" at other times. Since you want to be consistent, you can use the search and replace capability to change every "program" in the manual to "system." You can also search and replace selectively. If some occurrences of "program" should remain "program," the word processor can stop at each occurrence, and you can decide whether or not to replace it.

Your word processor may provide input to typesetting equipment. (See Chapter 26.) It may be able to produce graphs and charts to use as examples in the manual.

Spelling checkers are often available for word processors. These indicate misspelled words and allow the user to correct them. Some word processing programs check some of the grammar and semantics of the text. Some check for sexist words. All of these features can make the writing and editing tasks easier.

Summary   Know what features and capabilities exist and take advantage of them.

Use Word/Text Processing for Revisions

It is apparent that this capability is ideal for revisions. Only the changing parts of the manual need be typed. With a regular typewriter, the whole manual may have to be retyped.

Word or text processors are usually not page-bound. That is, if a change in the text affects page breaks, the word processor also changes the page breaks. That is impossible on a regular typewriter. Even typewriters that use magnetic cards as a storage medium are page-bound. One card stores one page.

Some equipment prints change bars to mark where text changed (Example 21.1). These are vertical bars in the right margin. They are useful during the review and update processes. (See Chapter 23.)

For example, the purchase order/inventory system may be updated to produce a document for verification of the purchase order for the Accounting Department. If we wanted to update the system overview of the functional specifications with that information, we could add it to the existing system overview and request that the word processor print the change bars.

If the word processing equipment available to you does not print change bars, draw them in with a pencil and a straightedge. Some word processors underline updated material. However, this may interfere with underlining in the text. For example, if you use the

Example 21.1   Updated Material with Change Bars

The system will produce the following reports:

Purchase orders listed by purchase order number

Purchase orders by date

Purchase orders by supplier

Purchase orders by item

Purchase orders received by item

Purchase orders received by check number

Purchase orders received by invoice number

Purchase orders received by supplier

Inventory items for re-order

Cost of items in inventory

Sales income from items sold

Cost compared with sales income

In addition to these reports, the system will print a purchase
order verification form for each purchase order entered. These
forms are for record keeping in the Accounting Department.

convention to underline user-entered data, underlining updated material will be very confusing.

Systems change and so must the manuals. When the manuals
are permanently stored on a word processor, updating is simplified.
The same things that make word processing helpful for revisions
make it helpful for updates. Some equipment can put the revision
dates on the updates automatically.

Use Word/Text Processing for the Index

Most equipment can search for specific words and phrases. This
capability makes creating an index easier than trying to find those

words and phrases yourself. Decide what items you want to include in the index. Find a word or phrase that describes each item. Then, use the search capability to find each occurrence of the word or phrase. Write down the page number of each occurrence. (The actual procedures will depend on your equipment.)

Use a Documentation Processor

Documentation processors are software packages that combine the technology of text processing with that of a data base. Creating user documentation using a documentation processor is practical when:

- a network of users is using an online application system.
- documentation can be all online; hard-copy manuals are unnecessary.

The first prerequisite for this method of creating user documentation is that you have the software available to you. The second is that you know how to use it.

If this method is practical and you meet the prerequisites, documentation processors offer many advantages. They provide a structured, yet flexible, design. They have skeleton Tables of Contents and preformatted text screens that prompt you through the creation of online documentation.

A documentation processor makes updating easier, because pieces of documentation are shared among and within documents. These pieces of text exist once, unduplicated. By updating a piece once, you update every spot in which it occurs.

Documentation processors, used in a network of microcomputers that have windowing facilities, can allow the users to view the user documentation and the application screen at the same time.

Programmers like documentation processors because the programmers are no longer required to be involved with help screens. Without a documentation processor, online documentation often becomes the responsibility of programmers. They code and maintain the help function and often write the text. A documentation processor makes the creation of user documentation independent of the application program.

Users like the online documentation that documentation processors provide. They have immediate access to the most current information about the application system by using a key or two.

PART III

After You Write

Just because a documentation is written and typed doesn't mean your work is completed. Now proofreading, editing, reviewing, and testing begin. The documentation is not in its final form yet.

Before it is completed, you must perfect the documentation (Section 7) and prepare it for release (Section 8).

Perfect the Documentation

At this point, you have a good draft that represents your best effort. But the documentation is not perfect. It still may contain typographical errors, inconsistencies, and technical errors. During this stage of development, clear up all of these imperfections.

To do this, you must proofread and edit the documentation (Chapter 22), review it (Chapter 23), and test it (Chapter 24).

22

Proofread and Edit the Documentation

Proofread the Documentation

Proofreading means checking for typographical errors, incorrect spelling, etc. This can be a tedious task.

Enlist Help   By now, you've become so familiar with the documentation that you know what is supposed to be there. Consequently, you may read things the way they *should* be and not the way they are.

Therefore, if possible, have someone else proofread the documentation. Often, a fresh viewpoint helps not only to spot mistakes but to point out omissions and illogical breaks in thought.

If time permits, two people can proofread together very effectively. You can read the longhand draft aloud while someone else reads the typed version. This ensures that nothing was omitted.

Use Standard Proofreading Symbols   Most typists understand proofreading symbols. These are shorthand ways of telling the typist how to correct the manual. Example 22.1 shows the standard symbols.

Example 22.1   Proofreading Symbols

Typographic Style

Set in <u>capitals</u>

Set in <u>small capitals</u> or <u>caps</u> and <u>small caps</u>

Mark	Meaning
(lc)	Set in LOWER CASE or ~~LOWER CASE~~ or LOWER CASE
(clc)	Set in CAPS AND LOWER CASE
(Init. cap)	Set in LOWER CASE WITH INITIAL CAP ONLY
(rom)	Set in roman type
(lf)	Set in lightface type
(ital)	Set in italic type
(bf)	Set in boldface type
(bf ital)	Set in boldface italic type

Punctuation Marks

Mark	Meaning
⊙	Period
ˆ,	Comma
ˆ;	Semicolon
⊙:	Colon
⸴	Apostrophe or single quote
ˇˇ / ˌˌ	Quotation marks
/?/ !/	Question mark; exclamation point
/ = /	Hyphen
(/)	Parentheses
[/]	Brackets
−⁄M	Em dash
−⁄N	En dash

Changes, Transpositions

Mark	Meaning
(tr)	Transpose characters
	Transpose the material circled
(stet)	Let it stand—all ~~material~~ above dots
/⌐/	Break line here
(run on)	Run on. Do not break line as typed
(sp)	Spell out 20 or Pres.

Insertions

Mark	Meaning
/added /⊙/	Insert words or punctuation

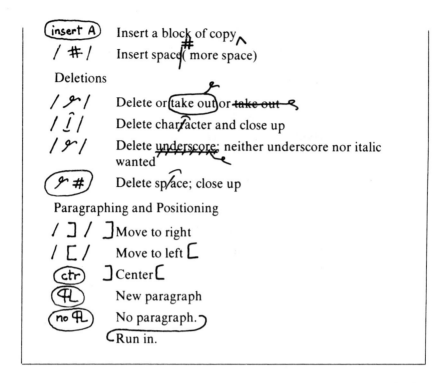

For dictated corrections, these symbols won't work, obviously. Learn how to correct dictated material. The instruction manual that accompanies the dictating equipment will explain error correction.

Edit the Documentation

Editing means reading the draft critically. Does something need to be explained in greater detail? Can you change passive voice verbs to active? Can long sentences be converted to two or more short ones?

Increase Clarity   One goal of editing is to increase clarity. As with proofreading, another person who is unfamiliar with the subject can point out items that are unclear.

Refer to the guidelines for clear writing in Chapter 9. Make sure you've followed those guidelines.

Insure Consistency   When you're writing a long manual, it is easy to use some words or terms inconsistently. Now that you have the entire manual, read it through. Make sure that not only words and terms are consistent throughout the manual, but that style and format are consistent.

Indentation should be consistent. Similar sections should use similar styles and phrasing.

Checklist for Editing the Documentation

1. Is the subject obvious from the beginning?
2. Is the manual complete?
3. Does it contain anything extra?
4. Is it well-organized?
5. Is it grammatically correct?
6. Are words spelled correctly?
7. Do most sentences have active voice verbs?
8. Are most sentences short but not choppy?
9. Is it technically correct?
10. Are computer terms explained?
11. Are abbreviations explained?
12. Does it fulfill its purpose?
13. Does it use consistent language and capitalization?
14. Is it visually pleasing?
15. Do the examples match the written instructions?
16. Are examples correctly placed?
17. Does the Table of Contents match the titles and headings in the text?

Revise the Draft   If you find enough errors in proofreading or enough changes result from editing, prepare another draft before submitting the manual to other people for their reviews.

23

Review the Documentation

Before documentation can be released, it always should be reviewed and usually should have approval signatures. Exactly who must review and approve it should be stated clearly in the written standards.

Once it is as good as you can make it, computer personnel and users must review it to make sure it is technically correct. Programmers and/or analysts will make sure that what you say the system will do is what the system actually does. Users will make sure that what you say about their subject area is correct.

Even after you've done all your research, you may still have some unanswered questions. Sometimes the best way to get the answers is through the review. Reviewers should spot incorrect or incomplete information.

For microcomputer applications, review procedures may vary. If you are developing documentation for a package that will be distributed to retailers, the procedures will be much different from those used if you are developing documentation for an in-house package. Apply the appropriate procedures suggested in this chapter.

Determine the Reviewers

Before you send copies of the draft to the reviewers, determine exactly who those reviewers should be. Perhaps not every programmer who worked on the system should review the manual. Maybe only the analyst or project leader should review it. Check with the person responsible for the system to find out who the best reviewers would be.

Likewise, not everyone in the user department or organization should review the manual. Determine who the best reviewers would be. Be careful not to offend anyone by omitting someone from the list of reviewers. Yet, limit the number of reviewers to between five and ten people, if possible.

Unfortunately, some system developers and manual writers do not have direct contact with the system's users. This is often true for time-sharing and software companies. In these situations, try to find a reviewer to represent the user. This should be someone familiar with the subject area but not with the system.

Provide for Multiple Levels of Reviewers

Many organizations require that executives have the final review. Programmers and users directly involved in the development of the system would review the manual first. When the manual satisfies those people, it would go to the executive level of review.

Often this executive review is a formality rather than an actual review. Schedule all the reviews and allow time for them when planning the release of the manual.

Establish Procedures for Incorporating Changes

No reviewer should feel that his or her comments went unnoticed. Therefore, if you do not make a suggested change, explain the reasons why.

Don't make any changes until all the drafts are returned to you. Then go through the manual page by page and incorporate the changes. If two or more reviewers make conflicting changes, do some research to determine the right change.

When all the changes are marked on one copy of the draft, retype the manual. On the new, revised version of the manual, mark all changed portions with vertical lines in the right margin. (See Example 21.1.)

Provide for Review of Changed Portions

Send the revised draft with change bars to all the reviewers. This time they need read only the changed portions. Return the reviewers' first draft also, so they can compare the first and second drafts.

Again, ask that these drafts be returned to you by a specific date. Review this second round of returned drafts as you did the first round.

If necessary, repeat the process until all reviewers are satisfied with the manual's content. After either the first or second round of drafts, try to arrange a meeting where all reviewers can discuss the manual.

Have a Sign-Off Sheet

When all the changes are made and all reviewers are satisfied with the manual, ask them to sign a sheet to indicate their approval of the manual.

Often the initial reviewers sign before executive reviewers. This assures executives that those people directly involved with the system have approved it.

Establish Review Procedures

Review is smoothest when governed by standard procedures. All reviewers should have a copy of these procedures. The nature and complexity of the procedures depend on the number of reviewers, the editing freedom of the reviewers, and the location of the reviewers. Location becomes important when the reviewers are in different cities and cannot meet face to face. This happens, for example, when a corporate headquarters develops a system to be used by its offices all over the country. Then, review procedures must cover how to resolve the questions and changes of long distance reviewers.

When location is not a problem, many review comments can

be handled in face-to-face meetings with all the reviewers present. This makes it easy to arrive at a consensus.

The review procedures themselves should be step-by-step instructions beginning with the first draft and ending with printing the final version of the manual. (See Example 23.1.)

Ask reviewers to make specific suggestions and changes. A question mark in the margin is not a very helpful review comment. Tell the reviewers how to mark their drafts. Give them a due date to return their drafts to you.

Example 23.1   Review Procedures

Reviewers

The minimum reviewers are:

the project leader in the user department
the project leader in the data processing department

Procedures
REVIEWER   1. Review the manual.
                 a. Make specific suggestions and/or changes.
                 b. Avoid comments such as "change this" or "wrong." Explain how it should be changed or why it is wrong.

              2. Return the manual to the author by the date specified.

AUTHOR   3. Consolidate all the changes.
                 a. Tell the reviewer why any changes were not incorporated.
                 b. Ask the reviewer about any vague comments.

              4. If there are several changes, prepare a second draft.

              5. Send the second draft to all reviewers.
                 a. Mark changed sections with change bars.
                 b. Return the reviewers' original drafts.

REVIEWER   6. Review the second draft, especially those sections marked by change bars. (See Step 1.)

7. Return the draft to the author by the specified date.

AUTHOR   8. Repeat Steps 3–5. Repeat this process as often as necessary to get a consensus.

9. Prepare a sign-off sheet.

REVIEWER   10. Sign the sign-off sheet when you are satisfied with the text.

AUTHOR   11. Prepare the final version of the manual.

12. Release the manual.

Checklist for Reviewing the Documentation

1. Determine the reviewers.
2. Have review procedures.
3. Put the reviewer's name on the draft.
4. Ask for its return by a specific date.
5. Consolidate changes when all drafts are returned.
6. Mark changes with change bars.
7. Return first draft with second draft to all reviewers.
8. Repeat the process until all are satisfied.
9. Sign off on the manual.

A final word of caution is important when discussing the review procedure. Be objective and open-minded. Most of us have some "pride of authorship" about our manuals. Accept the reviewers' comments as legitimate and honest attempts to make the manual better. They usually are. Their comments are rarely intended as personal insults.

24

Test the Documentation

No good programmer would release a program or system without first testing it. Since the user documentation is part of the system, test it too.

Provide for a User Test

Often the users supply data to be used in the system test. When they supply the data, have them use the documentation to complete the input forms. When they receive the output of the test, they should use the documentation to interpret the output, correct errors, etc.

In this way, you test the whole system and not just the computer part of it. Users get some practice before they go "live" with the system. They can tell you what they like and dislike about the documentation. If they have trouble with certain tasks, perhaps the documentation is unclear.

Make sure that the users understand the purpose of the testing phase. Ask them to keep a log of their comments and suggestions for both the computer system and the manual. Provide a log or form with questions to be answered. Try to make keeping the log easier than not keeping one.

Example 24.1 shows part of such a log for the purchase order/inventory case study. This example log is very general. Since you understand the users of the system, you may want to make the log more specific by providing alternative responses rather than asking for comments.

Example 24.1   Users' Test Log

```
Purchase Order/Inventory System
         User Test Log

Test Phase              Comments
ENTER Command:    Ease of Use: _____
                               _____
                               _____

                  User's Guide Explanation: _____
                               _____
                               _____

CHANGE Command:   Ease of Use: _____
                               _____
                               _____

                  User's Guide Explanation: _____
                               _____
                               _____
```

If users are not available, ask someone unfamiliar with the system to use it by using the documentation.

Test the Documentation Yourself

If users are unavailable for testing, try to use the system yourself following the instructions.

Another way you can test the documentation yourself is by using readability indexes. These indexes are based on word and sentence length; short words and sentences produce better readability scores. Indexes use formulas that provide quantitative, objective estimates of how easy the text will be for users to read.

Some states require that readability formulas be applied to certain types of material. For example, Pennsylvania requires that auto insurance policies pass a readability test. Thus, these indexes are accepted ways of helping writers insure that their readers will understand the documentation.

Many such indexes exist. Two of them are the Gunning Fog Index and the Flesch Reading Ease Scale. They measure reading skill and equate that skill to the number of years of schooling a person has had. Both Flesch and Gunning specify the number of years of schooling a person needs to understand something. Their reading indexes provide a way to measure this.

The Gunning Fog Index produces a score that equates a written passage's understandability to years of schooling. To use this index follow these steps.

1. Select a passage that is at least 100 words long.

2. Count the words. Count the sentences. Divide the total number of words by the total number of sentences. Round to the nearest whole number. This gives you the average sentence length.

3. Count all the words that have 3 or more syllables. Skip capitalized words (proper nouns), words that are combinations of short words (bookkeeper, for example), and words whose third syllable is "ed" or "es" (repeated, for example).

4. Add the average sentence length and the number of words with 3 or more syllables.

5. Multiply that sum by 0.4. The result is the number of years of schooling the person would need to read the passage easily.

Let's apply the index to the actual passage on diagnostic messages in Example 24.2.

Example 24.2   Using the Gunning Fog Index

Diagnostic Messages

As data are entered and processed, they are checked to assure the <u>accuracy</u> of the <u>processing</u>. When an error is detected, the error record will be printed at the <u>terminal</u> (or file if deferred or overnight <u>processing</u>) and the reason for the <u>diagnostic</u> given. In most cases, a special <u>character indicates</u> the "error" portion of the record.

Most <u>diagnostics</u> are explained fully with the <u>terminal</u> prompt; that is, the field in error is <u>identified</u> and the expected (or valid) values are <u>indicated</u>. In some cases, however, further <u>explanation</u> is <u>necessary</u>. This <u>appendix</u> provides a listing of all <u>diagnostics</u> that require further detail.

Use the steps described above.

1.   The passage is approximately 100 words long.

2.   It has 102 words and 6 sentences.

$$\frac{102}{6} = 17$$

Average sentence length is 17.

3.   15 words are 3 syllables or longer.

4.   17 (average sentence length)
     + 15   (long words)
       32

5.   32
     ×0.4
       12.8

12.8 years of schooling = college freshman

This level may be acceptable if all readers will have college educations. If this is not the case, the reading level is too high. Rewrite the passage. Example 24.3 is a rewritten version of Example 24.2.

Example 24.3   Using the Gunning Fog Index

Error Messages

The <u>computer</u> will edit data as they are entered. This assures <u>processing</u> <u>accuracy</u>. When the <u>computer</u> finds an error, it will print an error message at the <u>terminal</u>. The error message will explain the reason for the error. (If you selected deferred or overnight <u>processing</u>, the error messages will be on a file.) In most cases, a special <u>character</u> prints under the part of the record that is in error.

The <u>terminal</u> message explains the error fully. That is, the message <u>identifies</u> the field in error and lists the correct or valid entries for that field. In some cases, however, more detail is needed. This <u>appendix</u> lists error messages that require more detail.

Apply the index steps to the rewritten passage.

1. The passage is approximately 100 words.

2. The passage has 113 words and 9 sentences.

    $$\frac{113}{9} = 12\ 5/9$$

    Average sentence length is about 13.

3. 10 words are 3 syllables or longer.

4.   13   (average sentence length)
     $\underline{+10}$ (long words)
        23

5.   23
     $\underline{\times 0.4}$
       9.2

    9.2 years of schooling = high school sophomore

Anyone should be able to read this passage.

Other readability formulas are similar. Short words and sentences produce the best readability scores.

Unfortunately, we have no objective way to measure clarity of content. No surefire ways exist to guarantee that all readers will understand. Only users can provide that kind of feedback.

Summary   Use every means you can find to make certain the documentation is easy to read and understand.

Further References

Gunning, Robert. *The Technique of Clear Writing.* New York: McGraw-Hill, 1968.

Flesch, Rudolf Franz. *The Art of Readable Writing.* New York: Harper & Row, 1974.

Flesch, Rudolf Franz. *How to Test Readability.* New York: Harper & Row, 1951.
All these references contain ways to measure the readability of what you write.

Prepare the Documentation for Release

After complete reviewing and testing, the text is done. However, a few tasks remain before the printed manual can be sent to the users.

The writer's responsibilities may include preparing camera-ready copy and supervising the manual through the final stages of production. Sometimes another individual or department handles the production phases of manual development. Other times, the user manual is not printed; it is only typed and copied. Still, someone must be responsible for the production, whatever the scale of sophistication.

You must determine the manual's final form (Chapter 25) and prepare the final copy (Chapter 26). Section 8 (and most of Section 9) is applicable to printed manuals primarily.

25

Determine the Manual's Final Form

Many people think that all user manuals belong in loose-leaf binders. However, alternatives exist.

Use Binders

Binders are, of course, a common holder for user manuals. Use loose-leaf binders when frequent updates are expected or when the manual is over 200 pages.

Use dividers at the beginning of each chapter or section. Make sure the title on the divider matches the chapter or section title in the text.

If you use special binders that have the system name printed on them, order them well ahead of time. However, wait until you know the approximate number of pages in the manual so you'll know what size binders to order. (Binder size is measured by the size of the rings.) Have the name printed on the spine of the binder as well as on the front so the manual can be identified when it's on a shelf.

If your pages will be printed on both sides of the paper, make sure all chapters or sections begin on a right-hand page. Otherwise, the divider can't be used.

Binders are expensive. If a manual will be updated less than once a year and is shorter than 200 pages, it may be less expensive to reprint the whole manual in book form. This is especially true if the system is not expected to be in use more than 3 to 5 years.

Use Books

Bound user manuals can be less expensive, neater, and more compact than loose-leaf binders. However, unlike binders, bound books require sending the manual to a printer or to an in-house print shop.

Several kinds of bound books are possible: perfect binding, saddlestitching, and spirals.

Use Perfect Binding   Perfect bound means that the pages are glued together and the cover (front, spine, and back) is all one piece. The cover is glued on after the pages are glued together.

Use perfect binding when the manual is less than 200 pages and does not require section dividers.

If you use this method, allow for wider right and left margins on all pages. The whole book is trimmed after it is glued together.

Online systems often necessitate that the manual stay open while the user has both hands on the terminal. Therefore, perfect binding is inappropriate for such systems, because the manual will not stay open by itself.

Use Saddlestitching   Saddlestitched books have staples in the spine. (The signature held open at the fold resembles a saddle.) Use this only if the manual is less than 100 pages. For shorter manuals, it is an attractive and inexpensive method.

Use Spirals   We are all familiar with spiral tablets or stenographers' pads. Manuals can be bound that way too. Spirals can be plastic or wire. They work well for manuals as long as 200 pages.

Their advantage over perfect bound or saddlestitched books is that their spines will not crack, section dividers can be used, and the manual will stay open to any page.

The cover should be heavy paper and ⅛ inch bigger than the paper used for the contents.

Checklist for Manual Form

If the Manual Is	*Use*
longer than 200 pages	binders
updated more often than once a year	binders
less than 100 pages, not updated often	books—saddlestitched
less than 200 pages, not updated often	books—perfect binding or spirals

26

Prepare the Final Copy

Although the content is already finalized, the final original copy must still be perfected before it can be reproduced. Whether you copy the manual on a copy machine or send it to a printer, you must first add some finishing touches.

Finalize the Page Numbers

Only after the text is finalized can the final page numbers be added. After that, put the page numbers in the Table of Contents.

If the text makes reference to other parts of the manual by page number, put in those references now. (That is why it is better to refer to other parts of the manual by chapter or section title.)

Prepare Artwork or Graphics

Make sure that all examples, artwork, and other graphics will reproduce well and that they will fit in the spaces provided.

When someone else is preparing the artwork, the final versions may not have been part of the drafts. Therefore, before you can prepare the final copy of the manual, you must have final versions of all the artwork.

Copy the Manual

If you will be copying the manual on a copy machine, make sure that the manual will stay in the proper sequence. Since copying is often done with the pages face down, write the page numbers on the backs of the pages with a light blue pencil.

If you are using two-sided pages, figure out which pages are right-hand pages (odd-numbered pages) and which are left-hand pages (even-numbered pages). This is essential for the placement of examples. An example on the back of the page that has the instructions isn't as helpful as one that is across from it.

Knowing which are right- or left-hand pages is also essential if you use section dividers. The page that follows the divider must be a right-hand (odd-numbered) page.

After you've done this, you may have to manipulate or add text to avoid blank right-hand pages and to prevent any chapters with section dividers from starting on a left-hand page. (Blank left-hand pages are permissible.)

The effort involved in preparing two-sided pages may seem overwhelming. However, it is worth it when you consider that you cut your paper usage in half. If you can make a 200-page manual with 100 sheets of paper instead of 200 sheets and you make 20 copies of the manual, you've saved 2000 sheets of paper!

Use In-House Typesetting Equipment

If your company has its own typesetting equipment, take advantage of it. Typesetting allows you to produce more readable and attractive manuals. You have more type sizes and faces available to you.

A typeset page may also be more economical than a typed page that is copied. Typesetters give each character only the space it needs. Thus, more characters fit on a page. Fewer pages mean less paper and lower duplicating costs. If you mail manuals, fewer pages reduce postage and handling costs.

Typesetting has three basic methods:

Direct input

Tape

Computer typesetting

Direct Input An operator keys the text on a keyboard connected to the typesetter. Each character keyed appears on coated paper or film. The text is first printed on long galleys. These are long strips of paper to be laid out in pages as desired.

After the galleys are approved, they are pasted onto a layout page. The layout page is photographed. The photo negative creates an offset plate from which printing is done.

If this kind of equipment is available to you, you probably won't be involved in the keying. However, you may have the opportunity to help with the cutting and pasting for the layout. Thus, you can approve everything before it is photographed.

Tape Tape input can come from any compatible machine as long as the typesetter can read it. Optical character recognition (OCR) equipment can read typed pages and transfer the text to tape (punched paper tape or magnetic tape). The word processor may be able to provide diskettes for input.

Computer Typesetting This method is similar to some word processing systems but adds typographic capabilities to the editing capabilities. Computer typesetters recognize coding that tells them to change the type size, add white space, change to bold typeface, etc.

Many computer typesetters make input coding easier. They have programs that take word processing output and add the required codes. Then, operators need not have a great deal of knowledge about typesetting. They just need a good eye for size of type, captions, etc.

Sometimes "phototypesetting" and "photocomposition" are used interchangeably with "computer typesetting." Photocomposers set type as complete pages at high speeds.

Layout can be done on terminals. Thus, cutting and pasting before reproduction photography is eliminated.

Depending on the equipment's capabilities, you can be involved in the input and layout as one step.

Thus, if you have typesetting equipment available to you, learn how to provide input. Become involved in the layout. Know what the input and layout requirements are, so you can produce the finest-quality printed pages possible. Using the typesetting capability will make manual production faster than either typing/copying or using an outside printer.

Prepare the Manual for a Printer

Since most manuals sent to a printer use two-sided pages, all of the considerations about two-sided copy apply here.

Sending a manual to a printer is a little more work, but the improved quality is worth it. Therefore, if quality is important and you do not have in-house typesetting equipment, have the manual printed. Whenever a manual is for more than just in-house use, quality is usually more important.

You must provide the printer with camera-ready copy or material that can be converted for typesetting. The printer will define these requirements. The printer will first prepare galleys and/or page proofs for your review. The final step before printing is a brownline or blueline copy that is the final manual before it is printed. (These are called that because printers use brown or blue ink for this.) Review this copy before ordering the printing of the manual.

Summary   Use every means available to you to produce the highest-quality, most professional-looking, and easiest-to-use manual possible.

PART IV

After the Documentation Is Finished

At last! The documentation is done! You can breathe a huge sigh of relief! But, wait a minute! Maybe the bulk of your work is done, but you still have to release the documentation (Section 9). You also have to try to keep the documentation up-to-date (Section 10).

Release the
Documentation

Now that you have enough copies of the final version of the manual, you can release it. To do that, send the manual to the users (Chapter 27). Your responsibilities may also include conducting training seminars (Chapter 28).

27

Send the Manual to the Users

This chapter does not apply to manuals written for packaged software available through retailers, etc. For example, when a microcomputer package is completed and documented, the writer's job is done. The diskette (or cassette) and user documentation become one package to be sold.

When the users are in-house or known, however, send each user (or other people who should get one) a copy of the manual.

Include a Cover Letter

Especially if this is an in-house manual, send a letter or memo with the manual. The memo should be from you to all the manual holders. However, don't address it "TO: All Manual Holders." List all the names. In some cases, this may be impossible. If it is practical, however, use this device.

Example 27.1 Cover Letter for Releasing the Manual

From: Susan Grimm	Date: June 30, 1986
To: Janet Choi	Subject: Purchase Order/
Greg DuBois	Inventory System
Lucy Green	
Mark Jones	
John Lincoln	
Alicia Santos	

Enclosed is the user's guide for the new Purchase Order/Inventory System. The user's guide explains how to use the system.

Before you begin to use the system, we will have a training seminar. Please read the user's guide before the seminar. I will hold the seminar within a month. I will announce the seminar soon.

If you have any questions, please call me.

This will provide each manual holder with the names of all the other people who have manuals. It also gives all of them your name so they know where to direct questions.

Explain what the manual is and when to use it.

Keep a List of All Manual Holders

Whether you can write a memo and include everyone's name or not, it is essential that you know who has a copy of the manual. Otherwise, it will be impossible to provide the holders with updated materials.

Example 27.2   List of Manual Holders

Name	Date Issued	Returned
Janet Choi	6-30-86	_____
Greg DuBois	6-30-86	_____
Lucy Green	6-30-86	_____
Mark Jones	6-30-86	_____
John Lincoln	6-30-86	_____
Alicia Santos	6-30-86	_____
_____	_____	_____
_____	_____	_____
_____	_____	_____

Keep a list of those who receive the manual when you first release it. Update that list every time someone else orders a manual and whenever there are personnel changes. As new people request the manual, add their names to the list. If someone returns the manual, check the Returned column.

Summary   Make sure you always know who has a copy of the manual. Provide a way to keep track of manual holders and communicate to them.

28

Conduct Training Seminars

It is sometimes the responsibility of the manual writer to conduct or help plan seminars on how to use the system. This book is not a conference leader's guide or a teacher's handbook. Therefore, it does not explain *how* to conduct training seminars. However, it is a good idea to hold some kind of training seminar. Users can ask questions and get immediate answers. You can clarify points. It is important to use the manual during those sessions.

This will rarely apply if you write the user documentation for packaged software for microcomputers. However, retail computer stores frequently offer classes in the use of the computers and software they sell. Training is often part of the purchase price for other kinds of purchased software.

Plan the Seminar

Part of conference leading techniques involves organizing and coordinating the seminar. Plan what materials you will use and in what order you'll use them. Make notes for yourself about what you plan to say. But don't read those notes verbatim.

You have administrative duties also:

1. Get the room. Schedule it for the time needed.

2. Send out a memo announcing the seminar. (See Example 28.1.) In the memo, stress the need for attendance at each session if there is more than one.

3. Arrange for slides, tapes, or any other equipment.

4. Know how to run any machines, such as overhead projectors, tape players, etc.

5. Plan for emergencies. Have an extra light bulb for any projectors you use. Have plenty of chalk and a good eraser if you use a chalkboard.

6. If at all possible, provide hands-on experience with the machine and program.

Example 28.1   Memo Announcing an In-House Seminar

From: Susan Grimm   Date: July 12, 1986

To: Janet Choi   Subject: Purchase Order/
    Greg DuBois   Inventory System
    Lucy Green
    Mark Jones
    John Lincoln
    Alicia Santos

The training seminar for the new Purchase Order/Inventory System will be on July 26, 1986, in Conference Room B on the fifth floor at 9:00 A.M. The seminar will last all day.

Please bring your user's guide, which you received on June 30. Be prepared to discuss it in detail. Make a list of any questions you have.

If you have any questions about the meeting arrangements, please call me.

For a seminar that is not in-house, send a letter to the participants that explains the date, time, and location of the seminar. You should go into greater detail about the location since the participants may not be familiar with it.

Use the Training Manual

If the manual you have produced is a training manual, obviously it should be the basis for the seminar. Go through the manual from front to back. Use the case study examples. Develop exercises to allow the users to practice using the system.

Use the Reference Manual

Even if the manual is for reference, explain to users how to use the manual. Every time you explain something, tell the users where they can find that topic in the manual.

Use the Examples from the Manual

Reproduce the examples on overhead transparencies, slides, or posters. Explain how the examples relate to each step the user takes. Provide a different example also, if possible. Then, the user will have two examples to refer to and learn from.

Another advantage of using the manual in the seminar is the feedback about the manual it provides. You can pinpoint sections or concepts that are difficult to understand and revise the manual.

Checklist for Seminars

1. Devise a schedule and keep it.
2. Draw out the participants.
3. Encourage discussion.
4. Keep discussions to the subject.
5. Provide an opportunity for practice.
6. Provide feedback.
7. Don't criticize the participants or their current procedures.

Further References

Mager, Robert F. *Preparing Instructional Objectives.* Belmont, California: Fearon Publishers, 1975.

Nathan, Ernest D. *Twenty Questions on Conference Leadership.* Menlo Park, California: Addison-Wesley Publishing Company, 1969.
This is a concise, easy-to-read guide to conducting a seminar.

Update the Documentation

Documentation is never really complete. Even after it is released and the users are trained, you still must maintain it. Your job includes making sure that the documentation describes the system. If the system changes, the documentation must also change. To do that, you must establish update procedures (Chapter 29) and devise a way to determine if the documentation is up-to-date (Chapter 30).

29

Establish Update Procedures

When a user purchases software for a microcomputer, the program is on a cassette or diskette. Therefore, it does not change unless the user purchases or obtains a new version of the software and receives another diskette or cassette. The documentation writer updates the documentation for each new version of software, and an entire new manual (or other form of documentation) exists. Therefore, the update procedures in this chapter do not apply to that kind of software.

A user manual that does not describe the system accurately is useless. Often the system, and, hence, the user manual, remains the same for a long time. However, any system stored on a mainframe computer or written in-house for a specific application to serve a specific purpose or business need is subject to change. When a system changes frequently, keeping manuals up-to-date can be more of a problem than writing them. You must establish schedules and procedures for updating.

Will you issue updated pages or reprint the entire manual?

Will you issue updates every time a system change affects the user, or only periodically?

Will you have change bars in the margin to indicate changed material?

The answers to these questions depend on your situation. However, the following suggestions should help in any situation.

Issue an Update Whenever a Change Affects Use

Some system changes are not apparent to the user. Procedures remain the same. Other changes could affect use but the system can convert the old user input, for example, to the new requirements. However, if a system change demands new actions or procedures from the users, an update is essential.

Date Updates

On every updated page, put "Revised—10/86" or "Updated 10/86." If you use special stationery for your manuals, it may have

Example 29.1   Update Date on Manual Stationery

```
PURCHASE ORDER/INVENTORY   SECTION: Introduction
        USER'S GUIDE               PAGE: 1.4
                                   DATE: 6/30/86
                                   UPDATED: 1/15/87
```

The system will produce the following reports:

    Purchase orders listed by purchase order number
    Purchase orders by date
    Purchase orders by supplier
    Purchase orders by item
    Purchase orders received by item
    Purchase orders received by check number
    Purchase orders received by invoice number
    Purchase orders received by supplier
    Inventory items for reorder
    Cost of items in inventory
    Sales income from items sold
    Cost compared with sales income

In addition to these reports, the system will print a purchase order verification form for each purchase order entered. These forms are for record keeping in the Accounting Department.

a place for this date. Otherwise, put the date at the top or bottom of the page.

Example 29.2   Revision Date at Bottom of Page

The system will compute the total cost of goods sold and compare it with sales income.
The system will produce the following reports:

Purchase orders listed by purchase order number
Purchase orders by date
Purchase orders by supplier
Purchase orders by item
Purchase orders received by item
Purchase orders received by check number
Purchase orders received by invoice number
Purchase orders received by supplier
Inventory items for reorder
Cost of items in inventory
Sales income from items sold
Cost compared with sales income

In addition to these reports, the system will print a purchase order verification form for each purchase order entered. These forms are for record keeping in the Accounting Department.

Revised: 1/15/86

If you use a bound manual and reprint the entire manual, put the date on the cover.

Example 29.3   Revised Manual—Cover Page

PURCHASE ORDER/INVENTORY SYSTEM
USER'S GUIDE

June, 1987

(Revised and reprinted)

Use Change Bars

It is helpful to the users to know exactly what has changed. They may have gotten so accustomed to the procedures that they don't need to refer to the manual. Change bars point out what procedures are changing. (See Example 21.1 for an example of change bars.) When another update is needed, remove the old change bars and put in new ones.

For example, in the purchase order/inventory system case study, we may want to update the introduction to the manual. The system overview in the functional specifications is similar to the introduction in the user's guide. Since the functional specifications changed to add the purchase order verification, we should update the user's guide with that information.

Include a Cover Letter

Enclose a cover letter with the update. The letter can explain the changes. It should tell the user what to do with the update.

Example 29.4   Update Cover Letter

From: Susan Grimm	Date: January 15, 1986

To: Janet Choi
    Greg DuBois
    Lucy Green
    Mark Jones
    John Lincoln
    Alicia Santos
	Subject: Purchase Order/
	         Inventory System

This update to the Purchase Order/Inventory System User's Guide explains that the system now produces purchase order verification documents. The Accounting Department receives these verifications.

Remove and discard page 1.4 of your user's guide. Replace it with the attached updated page 1.4, dated 1/15/87.

Send the Update to Every Manual Holder

Use your list of manual holders that you developed when you re-leased the manual. Send everyone the updated material.

Summary   Use any of these methods or a combination to make sure that every manual on your distribution list is up-to-date.

30

Determine If
Documentation
Is Up-to-Date

You can have a complete list of manual holders and terrific updating procedures. But how can you guarantee that manual holders put the updates in their manuals? Obviously, you cannot. How can a new user determine if an old manual is up-to-date? That, too, is difficult. But some methods make it easier to determine if a manual is up-to-date. Since binders are the preferred form for frequently updated manuals, these methods apply to binders only. Bound manuals require that the entire manual be reprinted. Then, if the user has the new version, it is current.

Issue a New Table of Contents with Every Update

Every time you issue an update, reprint the Table of Contents. Next to the updated section on the Table of Contents, write "Updated 10/25/87." Then, users can compare the Table of Contents with the contents of the manual and see if it is up-to-date.

However, this still doesn't insure that the manual is up-to-date. What if an update were missed? A possible solution is to issue a new Table of Contents every 6 months even if there are no updates. Date the Table of Contents. Then, at least every 6 months, users can check their manuals against the Table of Contents that includes update information.

Example 30.1   Table of Contents with Updates Indicated

Table of Contents

Introduction
   Purpose of System 1.1
   Purchase Orders 1.2
   Inventory 1.2
   Processing 1.3
   Reports . . . . 1.4 (Updated 1/15/87)

Example 30.2   Dated Table of Contents

Table of Contents

June, 1987

Introduction
   Purpose of System 1.1
   Purchase Orders 1.2
   Inventory 1.2
   Processing 1.3
   Reports . . . . 1.4 (Updated 1/15/87)

Number the Cover Letters

Send a sequentially numbered cover letter with each update. Ask manual holders to file the cover letters in the back of the manual. Then, if they receive update number 3 and the last cover letter was for update number 1, they'll know they missed update number 2. They can then contact you and ask for the missing update.

Example 30.3   Numbered Update Cover Letter

From: Susan Grimm   Date: January 15, 1987

To: Janet Choi   Subject: Purchase Order/
      Greg DuBois   Inventory System
      Lucy Green
      Mark Jones
      John Lincoln   Update No. 1
      Alicia Santos

Update Number 1 to the Purchase Order/Inventory System User's Guide explains that the system now produces purchase order verification documents. The Accounting Department receives these verifications.

Remove and discard page 1.4 of your user's guide. Replace it with the attached updated page 1.4, dated 1/15/87.

File this cover letter at the back of your manual.

Issue a Current Contents Checklist

Periodically (once a year or after every 4 or 5 updates), send a list to every manual holder. The list would include each page of the manual and the date on that page. Users can check their manuals against the list (see Example 30.4). This method is similar to the Table of Contents method explained earlier.

Check the Manuals

If you have the opportunity, visit users' offices and ask if you may look at their manuals. Since you issued the updates, you can turn to a page that you know should be new. If it isn't, ask the user what happened to the update.

Such surprise checks may seem a little sneaky, but it is in everyone's best interest to have up-to-date manuals.

Example 30.4   Current Contents Checklist

From: Susan Grimm   Date: December 15, 1987

To: Janet Choi   Subject: Purchase Order/
     Greg DuBois   Inventory System
     Lucy Green
     Mark Jones
     John Lincoln
     Alicia Santos

Your Purchase Order/Inventory System User's Guide should contain the following pages.

Heading	Page No.	Date	Check
Introduction			
Purpose of System	1.1	6/30/86	
Purchase Orders	1.2	6/30/86	
Inventory	1.2	6/30/86	
Processing	1.3	6/30/86	
Reports	1.4	1/15/87	

If you are missing any of these pages, please complete the form below and return it to me.

I am missing the following pages:

Page	Date
_____	_____
_____	_____
_____	_____
_____	_____

Summary   All of these methods require two things:

1. A list of all manual holders
2. Cooperation from the manual holders

Any of these methods, or a combination, help, but do not insure, that manuals are up-to-date.

Glossary

Acronym Word formed by using the first initials of several words; for example, VSAM means *V*irtual *S*torage *A*ccess *M*ethod.

Action code Series of characters that define the type of processing requested; also called "transaction code" and "verb."

Active voice A verb used in a sentence so that the subject of the sentence performs the action described by the verb.

Analyst Individual who defines problems and finds solutions.

Batch A group of records for processing; processing groups rather than units.

Batch processing A computer system designed to be given batches of jobs from many users and see that they are all done.

Character One symbol, a number or a letter.

Code A system of symbols for representing data and instructions for a computer.

Command An instruction word that specifies an operation.

Computer file *See* File.

Computer graphics The use of a computer to define, store, manipulate, or present pictorial material.

Cookbook style The method of writing instructions with the verb as the first word in the sentence; so named because it is the style used in cookbooks for giving recipe instructions.

CPU *C*entral *P*rocessing *U*nit, the computer.

CRT *C*athode *R*ay *T*ube, terminal with a screen; also called "video display unit."

Cursor Indicator of the position on a CRT at which the next keyed character will appear.

Data Facts, numbers, letters, etc., submitted for processing.

Data base A method of storing data on the basis of the subject rather than the application. Data are stored independently from the programs that use the data.

Data dictionary   A listing of all the data that enter a system or are produced by it.

Decision table   Table that explains logical requirements and relationships by listing all possible conditions and actions.

Default   Data supplied automatically by the computer system when the user's data are missing or unacceptable.

Disk   A flat magnetic plate for storing data on a computer.

Documentation   A collection of information about a given subject whose purpose is to provide that information when and where it is needed in a form that is useful.

DOS   *D*irect *O*perating *S*ystem.

EOJ   *E*nd of *J*ob.

Ergonomics   The science that concerns itself with the health and safety aspects of the environment in which people and machines work together.

Error message   A message produced by the computer program that indicates an error has occurred.

Field   A set of characters treated as a whole.

File   A collection of related records treated as a unit.

File description   A technical description of the format and layout of a file.

Format   In a manual, the general plan of the organization or arrangement of text on the page.

Functional specifications   Detailed plans written to show clearly how the programs operate on the user's data to produce the desired results.

Galleys   Printed text that appears on coated paper or film.

Hardware   Physical equipment; *contrast with* Software.

Input   Data to be transferred to the computer.

Inquiry   Providing stored information on demand via a terminal.

Installation   A computer department and its computer hardware (machines).

JCL   *J*ob *C*ontrol *L*anguage; a language used by programmers to give the computer hardware operating system the specifications and instructions for a job.

Job stream numbers   Numbers assigned by data processing personnel to identify computer jobs or a series of jobs.

Light Pen   A device that looks like a pen and is used to input instructions to a computer.

Local terminal   Messages pass from CPU to terminal (and vice versa) along direct cable connections.

Logon *See* Sign on.

Logoff *See* Sign off.

Master file A file of information that is updated regularly and used as a main reference.

Microcomputer A computer smaller than a minicomputer or a mainframe (large frame) computer. It has a CPU (central processing unit), memory, input/output interfaces, and power supply. Like larger computers, it can accept data and operate on those data under the direction of programs.

Modem Data communication hardware that links processor and terminal to telecommunications network.

Mouse A candy-bar-size control unit used for computer input.

Noun A word that names a person, place, or thing; it is used in a sentence as the subject or object of the verb.

OCR *O*ptical *C*haracter *R*ecognition; The identification of graphic characters through the use of photosensitive devices.

Offline Description of activity done while not connected to the CPU.

Online Description of activity done while connected to the CPU.

Output Computer results.

Passive voice A verb used in a sentence in which the subject of the sentence is acted upon.

Playscript style The style of writing in which the actor is named, then the action.

Press type Letters that rub off a sheet onto the page.

Program A set of instructions that tells the computer how to handle a problem. A series of statements or actions that achieve a specific result.

Programmer One who prepares programs.

Program specifications Translation of the functional specifications into the functioning of the system; computer-related to explain the "how" of the system; describe distinct, separate tasks the system must perform; include design and logic requirements, program flowcharts, the purpose of each program, and other programming details.

Prompting message A message appearing on the terminal screen that prompts the operator to enter specific data.

Prose The ordinary style of writing (i.e., paragraphs, straight text).

Real time Simultaneously receiving information from several places and processing and returning it within a meaningful period of time.

Record A set of one or more consecutive fields about the same subject.

Recovery Restore files or data to a usable condition after system failure.

Remote   Separation of a terminal from its processor of enough distance to require telecommunications.

Report   Printed computer output.

Restart   Actions necessary to restore; reloading from a checkpoint.

Result table   Simple decision table which contains "if" (condition) and "then" (action) statements. *See also* Decision table.

Sign off   The process of breaking the connection with a time-sharing network.

Sign on   The process of accessing a time-sharing network; establish identity on a terminal each time contact is established.

Software   A set of computer programs and procedures that are concerned with the operation of a data processing system.

System   An organization of methods, procedures, techniques, people, and machines that interact to accomplish a specific function.

Tape   A strip of material that may be punched, coated, or impregnated with magnetic or optically sensitive substances, and is used for data input, storage, or output.

Telecommunications   The transmitting of messages between remote points.

Terminal   Computer peripheral capable of input or output of data.

Time-sharing   Many devices sharing the same computer and programs. Time available to each user is controlled by a central processor.

Topic sentence   The sentence that defines the main subject or topic of the paragraph using more detail than a heading. Usually the first sentence of a paragraph.

Voice   In grammar, the relationship between the subject and the verb.

Window   A part of a computer screen that allows the user to see parts of files. A user may look into more than one file or parts of the same file simultaneously by opening up more than one window on the screen.

Word processing   A system used for the production and maintenance of typewritten documents. Capabilities include:

retrieval of information

temporary or permanent storage of text

ordinary typing tasks

typing tasks difficult or not possible on an ordinary typewriter, such as:

moving text

copying text

inserting space/text within typed text

search and replace

NOTE: Capabilities vary with word processing systems.

Index